Andrew Doyle is a writse commentary on politicly published in the naticon *The Moral Maze* (BBC Radio 4) and often appears on Sky News. In 2019, he toured the UK with his stand-up show *Friendly Fire*. He is the author, as Titania McGrath, of the satirical books *Woke: A Guide to Social Justice* and *My First Little Book of Intersectional Activism*. He has a doctorate in Renaissance literature from the University of Oxford, where he also worked as a stipendiary lecturer. He was formerly a Visiting Research Fellow at Queen's University, Belfast.

Praise for *Free Speech And Why It Matters*

'Time was when the main threats to our free speech came from Mary Whitehouse, and the lawyer who in 1960 asked a jury whether they'd allow their wife or their servants to read D.H. Lawrence. But now it's the illiberal Left that would censor our words and police even our thoughts. One effective response to the new puritans is to laugh at them. Andrew Doyle does it brilliantly in the satirical guise of the lovely Titania McGrath. Now, writing as himself, he puts forward the serious case for free speech and why it matters. It isn't just serious, it's deadly serious. It really does matter' Richard Dawkins

'A fantastically timely book written by one of the smartest thinkers in Britain'
Piers Morgan

'Impassioned, scholarly and succinct'
The Times

'Doyle's book is terse, restrained and as carefully argued
as a QC's summing-up in a top-drawer courtroom drama
. . . a beautifully balanced and comprehensive overview'
The Critic

'*Free Speech And Why It Matters* is the primer that we
have been needing for some time'
Areo magazine

FREE SPEECH

And Why It Matters

Andrew Doyle

CONSTABLE

CONSTABLE

First published in Great Britain in 2021 by Constable
This paperback edition published in 2022 by Constable

5 7 9 10 8 6 4

A CIP catalogue record for this book
is available from the British Library.

ISBN: 978-0-34913-537-3

Typeset in Goudy by SX Composing DTP, Rayleigh, Essex
Printed and bound in Great Britain by Clays Ltd, Elcograf, S.p.A.

Papers used by Constable are from well-managed forests
and other responsible sources.

Constable
An imprint of
Little, Brown Book Group
Carmelite House
50 Victoria Embankment
London EC4Y 0DZ

An Hachette UK Company

www.hachette.co.uk

www.littlebrown.co.uk

For Jacques Berthoud

1935–2011

'Give me the liberty to know, to utter, and to argue
freely according to conscience, above all liberties.'

John Milton, *Areopagitica*

Contents

'We Need to Check
Your Thinking'

———

It's the kind of phrase that wouldn't seem out of place in the pages of a dystopian novel. Yet these were not the words of an agent of some totalitarian regime, but rather those of a police officer in the United Kingdom in 2019. Harry Miller, a fifty-three-year-old entrepreneur and former constable, was contacted by Humberside Police following a complaint by an offended party about a poem that he had shared on social media which was deemed to be transphobic. During the course of the conversation, the officer explained that, although not illegal, this nevertheless qualified as a 'non-crime hate incident'. Why, Miller asked, was the unnamed complainant being described as a 'victim' if no crime had been committed? More to the point, why was he being investigated at all? To which came the ominous response: 'We need to check your thinking.'

Over the past decade, many people have detected a pattern of minor changes in our culture, a kind of piecemeal reconfiguration at odds with our hard-won rights to personal autonomy. Miller's case is not an isolated affair. Between 2014 and 2019, almost 120,000 'non-crime hate incidents' were recorded by police forces in England and Wales. This sort of development has left a substantial number of us feeling as though we are no longer on secure ground; the tremors are too persistent. The 'culture wars', although often dismissed by commentators as a manufactured phenomenon, are closely tied to this gnawing sense that something is amiss. Miller's experience is one of many stories in which the principle of free speech has been casually disregarded for the sake of what is perceived to be a higher social priority.

Much of this can be explained by a sea change in the public's attitude to free expression and its key function in a liberal society. A new identity-based conceptualisation of 'social justice' has brought with it a mistrust of unfettered speech and appeals for greater intervention from the state. We are left facing that confusing and rare phenomenon: the well-intentioned authoritarian. When those who long for a fairer society are also calling for censorship, we find ourselves stranded on unfamiliar terrain. How are we meant to respond when the people who wish to deprive us of our rights sincerely believe that they are doing so for our own good?

Defenders of free speech are often confronted with the accusation that we are indulging in the 'slippery slope' fallacy. The occasional instance of state overreach, we are told, is hardly cause for alarm. Yet the idea that citizens of the United Kingdom might be investigated for 'non-crime' would have seemed unimaginable twenty years ago. One need only have a cursory familiarity with the history of authoritarianism to know that such regimes do not emerge overnight. I am by no means suggesting that we are freewheeling towards a future of gulags and show trials, but there appears to be a general degree of apathy that bodes ill for the preservation of our fundamental liberties.

Inevitably, the phrase 'Orwellian' has become something of a cliché and subject to derision by free speech sceptics, but it is predictable only because it is so pertinent. When Christopher Hitchens visited Prague in 1988 to report on the Communist regime, he was determined to be 'the first visiting writer not to make use of the name Franz Kafka'. During one of Václav Havel's 'Charter 77' committee meetings, police burst into the property with dogs and searchlights, threw Hitchens against a wall, and arrested him. When he asked for the details of the charge, he was told that he 'had no need to know the reason'. For all Hitchens's best intentions, the Kafka cliché was forced upon him. As he later observed, 'They make you do it.'

Similarly, cliché or no, the spectre of George Orwell looms large in current debates about freedom of expression. He joins a long line of thinkers who have explored what John Stuart Mill described in 1859 as the 'struggle between Liberty and Authority'. Opposition to free speech never goes away, which is why it must be defended anew in each successive generation. It is a privilege that has been denied to the overwhelming majority of societies in human history. Our civilisation is abnormal, almost miraculous, in its dedication to this most estimable of principles. Free speech dies when the populace grows complacent and takes its liberties for granted.

In 1644, the poet John Milton penned an elegant apologia for freedom of speech called *Areopagitica*, a counterblast to the

Licensing Order of June 1643 which would see all printed texts passed before a censor in advance of publication. Midway through his tract, Milton recalls meeting the elderly Galileo near Florence during his period of house arrest by the Inquisition. His crime was 'thinking in astronomy otherwise than the Franciscan and Dominican licensers thought'. The evidence of his studies had persuaded him of the validity of the Copernican theory of the earth's motion around the sun. Tellingly, Milton does not defend Galileo's views – at this time the Ptolemaic model of the universe was accepted by most educated people – but he clearly feels aggrieved at those authorities who would see the free-thinkers of the world punished and shamed.

History does not look fondly on the hubris of those who, like Galileo's inquisitors, appoint themselves as arbiters of permissible speech and thought. Their authority is only ever contingent on the wisdom of their time. Today's free speech sceptics are characterised by a similar tendency to mistake self-satisfaction for infallibility. If nothing else, the story of Galileo is a potent reminder of the importance of freedom of speech, and how none of us can ever be sure which heresies of today will become the certainties of tomorrow.

I start from the proposition that free speech is nothing less than the keystone of our civilisation. You may have reservations about this view. You may believe that unlimited speech enables the worst elements among us to commit harm. There is much to be said in favour of this perspective, although I hope to show you that a society that abandons freedom of expression risks exacerbating the very problems about which you are rightly concerned.

Left and Right

─────────

We have much in common. We would rather live in a world in which love and compassion triumph over hatred and bigotry. We believe that we have a responsibility not only for the wellbeing of ourselves but for those around us. We are troubled when people are mistreated, particularly for immutable characteristics over which they have no control. We feel that individuals should think before they speak and consider carefully the impact of their words.

All of which amounts to a substantial bedrock of shared values upon which we can build. Some are persuaded that these values are threatened by absolute freedom of speech. In this little book, I will try to show that the reverse is true, and that preventing individuals from expressing themselves as they see fit represents a far greater menace to social cohesion. If we agree on nothing else, we can at least accept that our goals are similar even if our views on how best to achieve them are not.

By acknowledging that our intentions are good, we are in a position to move forward and consider our differences and how these might be resolved. Too often these discussions are freighted with unfounded suspicion, mostly due to the belief that the defence of freedom of speech is associated with political extremism. Concerns over censorship are now routinely dismissed as 'a right-wing talking point'. As one commentator put it recently, there are those for whom free speech is 'nothing more than a political ploy, a ruse, a term the far right wilfully abuse to spread hatred'. In my view, free speech is a principle that transcends notions of 'left' and 'right' because all forms of political discourse depend upon its existence. Yes, unpleasant people are bound to use their speech to advance reactionary ideas, but the human right that enables them to do so is precisely the same right that allows us to counter them.

Moreover, if we permit the worst people in society to take ownership of our most fundamental values, we are gifting them a degree of power they do not deserve. Simply because hate-fuelled demagogues might disingenuously proclaim their fealty to free speech, this does not mean that the principle itself is tainted by association. Good people should not abandon their beliefs when bad people claim them for their own. If they do, such beliefs can only ever be said to have been tenuously held.

Free speech is the marrow of democracy. Without it, no other liberties exist. It is detested by tyrants because it empowers their captive subjects. It is mistrusted by puritans because it is the wellspring of subversion. Unless we are able to speak our minds, we cannot innovate, or even begin to make sense of the world. As Thomas Hobbes noted, the Greeks had 'but one word, *logos*, for both *speech* and *reason*; not that they thought there was no speech without reason, but no reasoning without speech'.

Free speech does not belong to anyone; it is a universal precept and a core human right. If it has come to be perceived as a specifically right-wing concern, this merely goes to show that those of other political persuasions have failed to uphold it. At any given historical moment, the defence of free speech is typically left to those who feel, justifiably or otherwise, that their opinions have become marginalised.

When I was a child, it was the right-leaning tabloids that would commonly call for censorship of television, film and the arts, whereas this is now predominately a feature of those who identify as being on the left. Similarly, the most vocal opposition to censorship today comes from right-wing commentators, whereas only a few decades ago the reverse was true. Misgivings about freedom of speech, then, cannot be said to be tied to any specific political allegiance.

To avoid the accusation of partisanship, it is therefore prudent to advocate consistently for the rights of everyone to speak freely, irrespective of whether or not we approve of what they have to say. In any case, the accusation is in and of itself an admission of bias. If we complain that our opponent's defence of free speech is some kind of subterfuge in order to advance a nefarious agenda, have we not already made a judgement about the validity of the position he or she intends to take? If our fear of free speech is that it facilitates the dissemination of bad ideas, then we have pre-emptively decided which ideas are beyond the pale. By doing so, we limit our own capacity to be challenged, and inadvertently reveal our existing prejudices.

Then and Now

———

The Ancient Greek notion of *parrhesia* is often translated as 'freedom of speech' but is better understood as 'speaking truth with candour'. The open and honest expression of viewpoints, however unpopular, was deemed essential to the business of Athenian governance. The Socratic Method – the drawing out of ideas through a dialectical process – was how arguments could be scrutinised and tested, even those deeply rooted in tradition. This was a progression beyond rigid hierarchies and helped to develop an egalitarian system of democracy.

Later, during the Roman Empire, the right to free speech in matters of politics was rarely extended beyond the Senate, although anyone familiar with Shakespeare will know that the plebeians could find ways to make their voices heard. The Catholic Church of the Middle Ages put an end to such privileges, ensuring that speech rights were the singular prerogative of men in authority. It wasn't until the invention of the printing press in the mid-fifteenth century and the subsequent spread of a new humanistic culture that freedom of expression was able to enjoy a resurgence in Europe. With the rediscovery of the literature of antiquity, and its sudden promulgation through the new printing technology, came the rebirth of *parrhesia*.

As the certainties of the past were gradually overturned during the Enlightenment, the struggle for free speech became paramount, and reached its apotheosis after the French Revolution with the *Declaration of the Rights of Man and of the Citizen* (1789) in which the 'free communication of ideas and opinions' was enshrined as 'one of the most precious of the rights of man'. The Reign of Terror (1793–94) meant that these liberties were short-lived, but with the First Amendment of the United States Constitution (1791), the notion of free speech was firmly embedded as a fundamental principle of Western civilisation:

> *Congress shall make no law respecting an establishment of religion, or prohibiting the free exercise thereof; or abridging the freedom of speech, or of the press; or the right of the people peaceably to assemble, and to petition the Government for a redress of grievances.*

The First Amendment is an acknowledgement that no institution is insusceptible to corruption. The Founding Fathers developed a system of governance with inbuilt checks and balances in order to countermand the possibility of malfeasance and the human thirst for power.

They understood, in other words, that free speech for all is the best defence against totalitarianism. It is the means by which we assert our self-determination in the face of those who might seek to control our behaviour, which is why dictators are quick to impose regulations on the press. After seizing power in 1933, Adolf Hitler's emergency 'Reichstag Fire Decree', sanctioned 'restrictions on personal liberty, on the right of free expression of opinion, including freedom of the press'. There is a good reason why writers of dystopian fiction portray their tyrannical regimes as hostile to free speech above all things. One need only think of the ruling party's imposition of 'Newspeak' in George Orwell's *Nineteen Eighty-Four*, or the 'firemen' of Ray Bradbury's *Fahrenheit 451*, eagerly ransacking houses for books to burn.

These bleak fantasies are too often reified wherever totalitarian regimes arise. The Founding Fathers doubtless envisaged something similar when they explicitly incorporated press freedom into the First Amendment. In recent years, there have been efforts to rein in the media, particularly in the United Kingdom, often in response to needlessly intrusive or even illegal conduct by journalists. While it is true that we must hold the press to account and insist on the highest ethical standards, strict press regulation inevitably benefits the most powerful in society. It is to the despot's advantage that his critics are muzzled. Even leaders with good intentions are prone to corruption when shielded from public scrutiny.

The First Amendment codifies a 'negative liberty'; that is to say, it affords citizens the right to freedom *from* government interference. While this is essential, it means that it is ill-equipped to tackle many of the free speech battles of the digital age. Historically, censorship has been enacted by the state, but with the rise of social media as the *de facto* public square, big tech corporations now have dominion over the acceptable limits of popular discourse. We are rapidly moving into an age in which unelected plutocrats hold more collective power and influence than any national government, only without any of the democratic accountability.

This is why the argument that private companies should be free to discriminate at will is is no longer persuasive or viable. They claim to be platforms committed to the principle of free speech, and yet at the same time behave like publishers who seek to enforce limitations on the opinions that may be expressed. Whenever the likes of Twitter or Facebook are sued for libellous material posted by their users, they invariably cite Section 230 of the Communications Decency Act, which ensures that they are not legally responsible for content that they fail to remove. The law was crafted out of an understanding that, given the proliferation of comment sections on news websites, it was always unfeasible to expect media outlets to be able to ensure that illegal content would not be uploaded. Yet now, this same law is routinely exploited to enable tech giants to censor with impunity. Worse still, the increased polarisation of politics means that many social media users whose views happen to align with big tech are cheering on the deterioration of their own freedoms because, for now, the impact is only being felt by their opponents. Tribal allegiances are blinding people to the long-term effects of corporate hegemony.

While it is true that social media companies have been subjected to governmental pressure to monitor 'hate speech' and 'fake news' on their platforms, there has also been a markedly paternalistic shift in the way in which their speech codes are formulated. Twitter, for instance, once saw itself as 'the free speech wing of the free speech party', and its CEO Jack Dorsey boasted that 'Twitter stands for freedom of expression', but a recent *New York Times* interview with the company's co-founder Evan Williams suggests that this commendable ideal no longer applies: 'I thought once everybody could speak freely and exchange information and ideas, the world is automatically going to be a better place,' Williams said. 'I was wrong about that.'

Inevitably, when tech giants now censor for overtly political reasons, their apologists repeat the mantra that in a free market economy 'a private company can do whatever it likes', including banning its users. While this is true, it does not mean they should escape robust criticism for their actions. Leaving aside the bizarre phenomenon of self-identified leftists calling for greater powers for faceless corporations, should this principle really be embraced? Should, for example, Facebook have the right to discriminate against gay people, or certain ethnic groups? Political orientation may not be an immutable characteristic, yet few of us would justify the suppression of political dissidents by the despots of history on these grounds.

Given the overwhelming left-leaning bias among employees in big tech, any efforts to police the tenor of conversation or 'fact-check' disputed news sources are bound to result in accusations of partisan censorship. These are not elected representatives invested with the authority to act on behalf of the *demos*, but multi-billion-dollar corporations who profit from selling our data to advertisers. If we are seeking moral stewardship, Silicon Valley seems an unlikely place to find it.

Those who claim that censorship can only be imposed by the state are making arguments that are over twenty years out of date. The Internet is the conduit through which ideas are shared in the digital age and, while sites such as YouTube, Facebook and Twitter remain dominant, we need to think carefully about how to ensure that free speech is not jeopardised. Irrespective of where you might stand on how best to address these problems, we can surely all agree that the global community is not best served by the cultivation of increasingly hermetic online 'echo chambers'. The last thing we need is for powerful corporations with an oligopoly on public forums to do our thinking for us.

Common
Misapprehensions

———

When defending freedom of speech, there are many misapprehensions that one is obliged to counter. I myself have often been accused of complaining that 'you can't say anything anymore', which is curious given that it is not a claim I have ever made. On the contrary, I have never been censored and do not believe it is likely to happen. I consider it a privilege to be able to express my views on radio, television and in print media, and take none of these opportunities for granted. Nobody is automatically entitled to a platform and, in spite of frequent suggestions to the contrary by free speech sceptics, it would be virtually impossible to find anyone who believes differently.

The cliché of 'you can't say anything anymore' is, in fact, most frequently iterated by those who are criticising an imaginary enemy. Whether this is tactical or not, there is a clear tendency among those who oppose unlimited speech to misrepresent what others have said in order to denounce them.

With the exception of the occasional clickbait tabloid article, 'you can't say anything anymore' is not a phrase that is in common currency. Even on the rare occasions that the phrase is used, it is never meant literally, but rather as a hyperbolic way of articulating frustration at the creeping encroachments on free expression that are there for all to see. The hyperbole is self-evident; after all, by saying 'you can't say anything anymore' you are discrediting the point in the very act of speaking.

Another common misapprehension levelled at free speech advocates runs along the lines of 'Why are you criticising this person's opinion? I thought you supported free speech?' One can only assume that those who mistake criticism for censorship are doing so wilfully. The act of refusing to engage in discussion is often similarly misinterpreted. Helen Pluckrose and James Lindsay call this 'the fallacy of demanding to be heard'. Just as freedom of religion incorporates freedom *from* religion, the right to speak and listen also entails the right *not* to speak and listen.

One of the more insidious misconceptions is that those who argue in favour of free speech simply do not care about minorities, or even wish to return to a time when casual racism, homophobia and sexism were ubiquitous. According to this supposition, the very notion of freedom of speech is a 'dog whistle', a term typically deployed when the target of a critic's ire has not said anything incriminating, but a pernicious underlying intention is nonetheless assumed. This is a hypothesis explored in Gavan Titley's book *Is Free Speech Racist?* (2020), in which it is posited that freedom of speech 'has been adopted as a primary mechanism for validating, amplifying and reanimating racist ideas and racialising claims'. It is a great shame that we now live in a world in which something as honourable as defending free expression can so often kindle dishonourable suspicions.

Racism is a cancer that can never be tolerated in a civilised society. There are doubtless some defenders of free speech who harbour racist views but, thankfully, they form a negligible minority. My experience of working with anti-censorship campaigners is that they are invariably opposed to all forms of prejudice, and that their passion for freedom of expression is largely driven by the desire to protect the rights of the most vulnerable in society. As the work of human rights campaigner Jacob Mchangama has shown, the suppression of minority rights is most acute in countries where free speech protections are meagre.

It is undeniably the case that the cause of free speech has occasionally been taken up by some of the most reactionary characters in society. This is to be expected, given that what they have to say is not only unpopular, but is also guaranteed to cause widespread consternation. Defending free speech means defending the rights of those whose speech we despise. Uncontroversial ideas require no such protection.

When we stand up for the speech rights of repellent figures, we inevitably leave ourselves open to the accusation of complicity. To assume that defending another's right to speech is a form of approval of its substance is a grave error that discourages many of us from upholding the principle. The majority of those who oppose the criminalisation of racist speech do so precisely because they abhor racism. They would prefer such individuals to be challenged and, if possible, shown how their prejudice is fundamentally irrational. While it is true that most of us, myself included, lack the patience and the ability to talk anyone out of his or her racist delusions, the likes of Daryl Davis – a musician who has successfully deradicalised numerous members of the Ku Klux Klan – prove that it is possible.

Racism would not magically disappear if society were to suppress all forms of racist speech. Instead, it would preclude the possibility of any form of public counter-argument. Expert reconciliators such as Davis would be redundant, leaving the racists to flourish in the shadows. Of course, one could rebut this view by suggesting that the suppression of racist speech in and of itself prevents further radicalisation. Seen in this way, we are faced with the utilitarian question of which course of action leads to the greatest good for the greatest number.

On balance, I am persuaded that the dangers of empowering the state to determine the limitations of expression far outweigh the risk of small groups of extremists attempting to proselytise. The cost of freedom is that it is open to abuse by an unconscientious minority but, once liberty is relinquished, it is difficult to recover. To those who would trust the state to monitor our speech, I would remind them of Thomas Paine's closing remark in his *Dissertation on First-Principles of Government* (1795): 'He that would make his own liberty secure, must guard even his enemy from oppression; for if he violates this duty, he establishes a precedent that will reach to himself.'

Let us consider a specific example of how good people have been instrumental in defending the speech rights of those with unpardonable views. In 1977, in the suburb of Skokie in Chicago, a group of neo-Nazis were banned from marching by the city council. On the face of it, the decision made sense; nearly half of Skokie's population was Jewish, including hundreds of survivors of the Holocaust. The demonstration appeared to be no more than anti-Semitic provocation for its own sake.

To the surprise of many, the American Civil Liberties Union (ACLU) came to the defence of the neo-Nazis. While this seems counterintuitive, it was a true test of the organisation's commitment to constitutional freedoms. The question was not whether the bigotry of neo-Nazis had any basis in truth, but rather to what extent free speech is an indivisible liberty. Is it for everyone, or exclusively for those who espouse morally justifiable ideals?

The ACLU understood that to make exceptions for the neo-Nazis would be to dilute the principle, thereby setting a precedent that threatens the rights of all of us. A detailed account of the case was written by Aryeh Neier, a Jewish refugee from Nazi Germany who served as National Director of the ACLU from 1970–78. In his book, *Defending My Enemy* (1979), he explains that he 'supported free speech for Nazis when they wanted to march in Skokie in order to defeat Nazis'. For Neier, the conservation of his adversary's First Amendment rights was 'the only way to protect a free society against the enemies of freedom'. The recent conception of 'hate speech' is, in effect, a kind of fudge that attempts to circumvent this moral quandary. We might label speech we despise to be 'hateful' and therefore not subject to constitutional protection, but we have merely redefined the terms in order to evade an uncomfortable moral obligation to defend its existence.

The counter-argument is that once a society has reached a consensus that certain practices are inherently evil – Nazism and slavery being the most obvious examples – then there is no risk in proscribing speech that champions the indefensible. But the content of the speech itself, however emotive, is beside the point. The question we must ask ourselves is not whether we should support the speech rights of neo-Nazis, but whether we wish to entrust the state to put such strictures in place. The authoritarian regimes of the past show us that once such powers are granted, they can be injudiciously applied in ways that were never anticipated.

For instance, after what become known as the 'Battle of Cable Street' on 4 October 1936 – where Oswald Mosley's 'blackshirts' were intercepted by anti-fascist demonstrators as they attempted to march through the East End of London – the Labour party was instrumental in urging parliament to rush through Public Order legislation to stop further uprisings by the far right. Yet since their inception, these measures have mostly been used to clamp down on left-wing activism, and formed the basis of the Government's justification to arrest striking miners in the mid-1980s. By granting the state the legal powers to ban fascist marches, the left had inadvertently stymied its own cause.

There is no contradiction in holding individuals in contempt for their repugnant views and simultaneously defending their right to express them. The fallacy of guilt by association is a pervasive feature of today's discourse, both online and in the mainstream media. Little wonder, then, that most people would rather stay out of such discussions altogether than risk being yoked to disreputable characters.

This is why those of us who believe in free speech have a duty to be clear when we disapprove of the speech we are defending. Standing up for the rights of the worst people in society comes at a great personal cost. The task is less onerous if we are able to communicate the message that we do not protect controversial speech for its content, but rather the principle it represents.

The Social Contract

'Everyone has lines that can't be crossed,' says journalist Yasmin Alibhai-Brown. 'There are always degrees of permissiveness, with cultural as well as legal limits that are so familiar we barely notice them. Claims about the inviolability of free expression are humbug.' To an extent, she is right. We all have individual standards by which we abide, and this includes limitations on the ways in which we choose to express ourselves.

Where Alibhai-Brown errs is in failing to make a clear distinction between voluntary and compulsory restraint, one that is mirrored in the distinction between the cultural and legal limits that she mentions. The social contract is an ever-evolving, broadly accepted consensus that will always have its dissidents. We agree to the accustomed conditions of politeness, but do not surrender our right to ignore them without risk of arrest or prosecution. Any legal barriers to speech deprive us of that agency, and outsource our personal responsibilities to the state.

I use the term 'social contract' not necessarily to invoke Rousseau's conception of the general will as the moral basis for the law, but rather as a shorthand for the essentially co-operative nature of human society that he describes. Just as the law is the apparatus by which we reconcile our individual freedoms with the authority of the state, decorum is how we achieve rapprochement between citizens who have competing priorities and instincts. Yet the two remain distinct; decorum can never be legally binding, which is why Alibhai-Brown's conflation of cultural and legal constrictions is somewhat specious.

There is a further distinction, rarely understood, between 'hate speech' laws which dictate that a citizen may not transgress the voluntary social contract, and legislation that prohibits speech as a *means* to commit a crime. Laws against fraud, libel, perjury, blackmail and espionage are not violations of one's freedom of speech. These are examples of where speech has operated as the mechanism of criminal activity, but is not the crime itself. Speech is to perjury what fire is to arson. Certainly we can use words to commit crime – the same could be said of almost anything: water, bricks, golf clubs, even stuffed halibuts – but in a murder case we punish the killer, not the weapon. Yes, there are sensible restrictions on dangerous devices or substances, but speech is integral to the human spirit and hardly comparable with guns, knives and poison. It would take quite a pessimistic leap of the imagination to suppose otherwise.

We see a similar misunderstanding in the most revered maxim of those who distrust freedom of expression: 'You can't shout "Fire!" in a crowded theatre.' The saying originated in the 1917 United States Supreme Court ruling against Charles Schenck, a socialist who had issued a broadside calling for young men to refuse military conscription and was convicted under the Espionage Act. It was Justice Oliver Wendell Holmes who wrote the statement: 'The most stringent protection of free speech would not protect a man in falsely shouting "Fire!" in a theatre and causing a panic.' This has since been appropriated as pro-censorship boilerplate, but on further examination the argument collapses.

First, something has been lost in the misquotation. Holmes was specifically referring to needless panic-mongering, which is why he wrote of 'falsely shouting "Fire!"'. At some point in its transition to a modern-day proverb, the word 'falsely' was dropped. This is a peculiar alteration, given that we all accept that if an actual fire were to be spotted in a crowded theatre, it would not only be our right to shout 'Fire!' but a moral obligation.

Second, this was never a legally binding statement. Holmes merely used the analogy to justify upholding Schenck's prosecution. As Gabe Rottman has noted, the 'crowded theatre' argument is 'worse than useless in defining the boundaries of constitutional speech' because as a metaphor 'it can be deployed against *any* unpopular speech'. The incoherence of Holmes's position is why the decision of the court in *Schenck v. United States* was overruled in 1969. It is now regarded as an egregious error in judgement, which makes it a somewhat frail basis for advancing the case for censorship.

Besides, there is nothing to prevent us from falsely shouting 'Fire!' in a crowded theatre but, having done so, the proprietors would be well within their rights to eject us from the premises. In buying a ticket to a public performance, we have tacitly entered into a contract to behave in a manner that does not detract from the enjoyment of others. By extension, we have already consented to be removed if we breach that agreement. Needlessly generating a panic in which people are likely to be hurt clearly falls into this category. The crowded theatre analogy is misleading because the scenario it describes is unrelated to the issue of free speech.

Ultimately, the subjective nature of offence means that we must each draw our own boundaries for what we consider acceptable forms of expression. If we choose to transgress the limitations favoured by the majority, we are likely to be criticised, harangued and ridiculed. But such responses are the prerogative of those who are exercising their free speech as a rebuttal to our own. This is, after all, how the social contract is developed and maintained.

Criticism is not the same as censorship. Infractions against free speech generally occur when one party resorts to harassment or threats in order to silence the other – a common feature of today's 'cancel culture' – or if the state attempts to criminalise those who deviate from the popularly accepted thresholds of polite expression. We all have a right to incivility, just as we have the right to opinions that are considered to be beyond the purview of permissible thought. Likewise, those who wish to criticise such forms of dissent are free to express their disapproval however they see fit within the law. This is the liberal system, and it works.

Cancel Culture

––––––

'Cancel culture' is a shorthand metaphor for a retributive method of public shaming and boycotting, often for relatively minor mistakes or unfashionable opinions, which is typically driven by social media. Those who support the tactics of cancel culture have been known to deny its existence, claiming instead that they are merely holding the powerful to account. However, the key difference is that when it comes to cancel culture, targets are denounced rather than criticised, and the consequences are hugely disproportionate to the perceived slight. Often, complaints are addressed directly to employers in the hope of depriving the target of his or her livelihood. This is why the victims of cancel culture tend to be ordinary people who do not have the kind of financial resources to protect them from such campaigns.

The practitioners of cancel culture habitually engage in what is known as 'gaslighting', a term which denotes the act of flatly contradicting observable reality. They smear their targets as 'bullies' as a means to bully them, or cast themselves in the role of victim while they victimise others. Often, this is achieved by claiming that they have been made to feel 'unsafe' or that 'violence' has been inflicted, which is usually enough to ensure that the target will lose his or her job. After all, an employer will not fire someone for a simple matter of disagreement, but will be obliged to take action if 'harm' can be said to have been caused. Even the denial of cancel culture itself is a form of 'gaslighting', because it requires that we ignore the overwhelming evidence of its existence.

When a group of well-known figures – including Margaret Atwood, Noam Chomsky, JK Rowling and Salman Rushdie – published an open letter in *Harper's Magazine* decrying this new climate of intolerance, the backlash was intense. The relative privilege of the signatories was held up as confirmation that cancel culture is a myth, and that these rich celebrities were simply unaccustomed to having their views disputed. This, of course, is to miss the point spectacularly; it was precisely their financial security that enabled them to sign the letter in the first place.

A particularly germane example is that of the writer JK Rowling, who has been subjected to an unrelenting campaign of mischaracterisation for expressing concerns about the possibility that gender self-identification might compromise women-only spaces such as domestic violence refuge centres. She has explicitly pledged her support for equal rights for trans people, but some have nonetheless interpreted her views as hostile. In particular, Rowling's conviction that there is a biological basis to womanhood, one shared by the majority of the population as well as the scientific community, has angered activists. In spite of broad support from many trans individuals, a vocal minority have bombarded her with abuse of a sexually threatening nature.

Social media has a tendency to distort the truth, to amplify the loudest and most obnoxious marginal voices. Needless to say, those who are engaging in harassment, or burning copies of Rowling's books and posting the footage online, are by no means representative of the trans community. At the same time, in the midst of the hysteria there has been little opportunity for sober discussion of the issues, and many people have been discouraged out of fear of reprisals. Cancel culture does not seek to criticise, but to punish, and leaves little scope for redemption. This is why the singer Nick Cave has described it as 'mercy's antithesis'.

Like the other signatories to the *Harper's* letter, Rowling has been held up as an example of the erroneousness of cancel culture. 'JK Rowling isn't being cancelled,' claimed one journalist, 'she's just facing the consequences of her actions,' a position that cuts close to sanctioning harassment. While it is true that Rowling's agent and publisher have defended her right to free speech, it is doubtless the case that a less lucrative client would not have fared so well. In July 2020, children's book author Gillian Philip was dropped by her publisher simply for supporting Rowling. Rather than disproving the reality of cancel culture, Rowling's circumstances demonstrate that it is the least powerful who are the most vulnerable to its effects.

A typical complaint about those who are pushing back against cancel culture is that they are attempting to silence their critics. 'Too often', writes Owen Jones, 'people seem to think freedom of speech means "saying things without being challenged by others who are also using their own freedom of speech"'. Likewise, Nesrine Malik claims that many have succumbed to the view that 'freedom of speech means freedom from objection'. In her book *Why I'm No Longer Talking to White*

People About Race (2017), Reni Eddo-Lodge feels obliged to declare that free speech 'doesn't mean the right to say what you want without rebuttal', thereby countering an argument that no serious person has ever made.

It is simply not credible to suggest that the belief that 'freedom of speech means freedom from consequences' is anywhere near as commonplace as these writers assume. Unpleasant speech can provoke scorn, ridicule and even ostracism, none of which constitutes an infringement of human rights. It is only when speech is met with threats, censorship, defamation, harassment, intimidation, violence or police investigation that freedom becomes compromised. These are the tools of cancel culture.

Denials of cancel culture are difficult to fathom given that stories about people who have been hounded out of work for causing offence so frequently appear in the national media. Inevitably, studies now show that many are choosing to self-censor in order to avoid the wrath of the online mob. A recent survey by the Cato Institute and YouGov found that nearly two-thirds of Americans feel compelled to keep their views to themselves out of fear of causing offence, while a third are refraining from sharing their political opinions because they believe their employment prospects would be endangered if they did so.

There are few of us who do not know people who have lost work, been disciplined or been passed over for promotion on the grounds of relatively innocuous remarks they have made in a private capacity. Even towards the end of my former career as a teacher, many of my colleagues had given up on making jokes in the classroom because they understood that deliberate misconstructions of their words could be used against them by pupils or parents with a personal grudge. The result was an enervated and less stimulating learning environment, and all it took was a few pupils to make disingenuous complaints to ruin it for the rest of them. This is now an accepted feature of all modern workplaces, only it is adults who are generating these precarious conditions. When people are expected to behave like robots, who will never misspeak or inadvertently cause offence, the business of living is reduced to drudgery.

It only takes a few instances of 'cancellation' in any given workplace to create the kind of atmosphere in which remaining employees are intimidated into toeing the line. This is not a direct violation of free speech – companies are entitled to insist on speech codes, and those who work for them are entitled to resign if they disapprove – but frequently employers are capitulating to complaints that have been made maliciously in order to punish people for their opinions rather than any genuine breach of contract.

The full scope of cancel culture is difficult to estimate because its purpose is to foment an all-encompassing attitudinal shift. Like 'No Platforming' – the practice of denying platforms to individuals with controversial views – most of the targets of cancel culture are pre-emptive. University student unions are able to claim that they never ban or disinvite contentious speakers, precisely because such individuals would never be approached in the first place. This is not to suggest that anyone has a right to a platform but, in these cases, the regulations set by a few powerful committee members have effectively torpedoed the possibility of other students being exposed to a diverse range of guests.

Similarly, cancel culture works by an unwritten rubric. The job losses and public shaming are merely the visible manifestations of a broader problem. Many who are judged guilty of committing thoughtcrime are simply disqualified from opportunities for future work and, in most cases, will never even know. Like an ex-convict whose former transgressions hamper him from ever finding meaningful employment due to criminal disclosure checks, anyone who has ever expressed an unfashionable opinion on social media is likely to be scuppered by the most cursory of Internet searches.

In 2020, the journalist Helen Lewis was hired by Ubisoft to record dialogue for their video game *Watch Dogs: Legion*. When the company was alerted to Lewis's writings on gender identity – nuanced and compassionate, but not wholly in line with current intersectional trends – her voice was erased from the game and an apology was issued. This is how cancel culture works; it takes little more than a few tweets from activists before corporations relent to their demands. It is the heckler's veto writ large. Lewis is the visible casualty of 'cancellation' in this instance, but the invisible casualties are those candidates whom Ubisoft will veto in future for the crime of holding impure thoughts. As the company stated: '[We] will reinforce our background checks for partners in the future'.

The Indispensable
Condition

It is no coincidence that cancel culture has developed in tandem with a rise in scepticism about freedom of expression. To an extent, this comes down to a generational divide. Studies have confirmed that younger people today are more likely to favour government-enforced restrictions on speech. In other words, they tend to perceive freedom of expression as being in conflict with minority rights and are willing to see it compromised for the sake of a more inclusive society.

It is my contention that any such conflict is illusory, and that free speech is the only way to ensure that marginalised people are heard. To set limits on speech in order to improve tolerance is like attempting to extinguish a fire with gasoline. It infant- ilises those who are singled out as requiring insulation from distressing ideas, undermines the principle of equality under the law, and frustrates the means by which injustices in society can be effectively overcome. Moreover, tolerance is a virtue that requires an acknowledgement of disapproval. It means that we are able to support the rights of others to hold opinions we cannot respect. This is the liberal ideal.

Those who demand respect are, in effect, insisting on deference. The idea that certain beliefs ought to be ring-fenced from criticism and ridicule is the very antithesis of liberalism. In any case, how we determine who might qualify for such special protection will very much depend upon the subjective judgement of those in power at any given moment. For instance, there are many who argue that the perceived rise of Islamophobia might be redressed with prohibitions against the criticism of Islam. They have forgotten that the very same logic could be applied by unscrupulous governments of the future who wish to avoid being held to account. We should be wary of short-term remedies which may provide the ready-made tools for state-imposed censorship.

In an age when 'lived experience' is often valued more than objective truth, the core tenets of liberalism – due process and free speech – are bound to be at risk. 'Lived experience' is what we used to call 'anecdotal evidence', a fallacious form of reasoning that has misled many into believing that ours is an essentially oppressive society, overrun by fascists and undergirded by white supremacy. Needless to say, those whose 'lived experience' tells them that this worldview bears little resemblance to reality are quickly discounted. It would seem that 'lived experience' only matters if it is of the approved kind.

As ever, there is a kernel of truth in the lie. Fascism has by no means been eliminated, and studies have suggested that the far right is experiencing a resurgence. While this is undeniably concerning, the same evidence also tells us that such sympathies remain very much at the periphery. Those who insist that fascism has become normalised have a tendency to discard, or entirely misrepresent, statistics that do not reflect their pessimistic view.

An emphasis on the importance of diversity makes sense because of historical discrimination, so it is a great shame that social justice activists have so consistently failed to defend diversity of opinion. True progressives understand that without freedom of speech – and, by extension, freedom of thought and conscience – nothing else can be achieved. The civil rights luminaries of the twentieth century, who fought for black emancipation, gay rights and women's suffrage, all recognised that without freedom of speech theirs was a lost cause. They embodied the memorable words of Benjamin Cardozo, Associate Justice of the United States Supreme Court from 1932–38, who described freedom of expression as 'the matrix, the indispensable condition, of nearly every other form of freedom'.

At a time of endemic oppression, it was only through speech and protest that the societal mechanisms for the emancipation of minorities and women could be actuated. This is why the Free Speech Movement at the Berkeley campus of the University of California in 1964 was such a turning point, and is so often discussed in relation to the struggles of contemporaneous civil rights campaigns and the New Left. One of the movement's leaders at Berkeley, Mario Savio, extolled freedom of speech as 'something that represents the very dignity of what a human being is'. For those of us who genuinely care about equality, the reinstatement of this principle ought to be a priority.

With contemporary politics now dominated by issues of identity, it is sometimes difficult to detach the arguments for and against freedom of speech from the person who is making them. Too often, opinions are dismissed through various forms of *ad*

33

hominem assessments. Some people believe that if hateful speech has a disproportionate impact on minority groups, then those with perceived 'privilege' are less entitled to opine on the subject. This is why a defence of free speech by a straight, white male is likely to be met with the objection that he is unqualified to apprehend the potential harm of words. But when the same arguments are advanced by a black lesbian, as they so often have been, there is nowhere left for the identity-fixated critic to retreat. Put simply, if you frame your counter-arguments in terms of the immutable characteristics of the person you oppose, you are setting yourself up for failure. At the same time, you obfuscate the actual issue in question.

While it is true that there are invaluable insights to be gained from personal experience, this approach makes all kinds of assumptions. The first is that any one form of privilege – most commonly racial, sexual or gendered – should be deemed more advantageous than another, a proposition that is only possible to support in the most abstract terms. The notion that an individual's privilege can be reasonably quantified and allotted into some kind of hierarchy is essentially unsound. There are too many variables to take on board, many of which cannot possibly be known without a comprehensive understanding of each person's background and circumstances.

Even if such a feat were possible, would there be any merit in dismissing an argument on the basis of the person who made it? Quite apart from the fallacy of assuming bad faith, a condition of open and productive dialogue is that the thoughts expressed are evaluated independently of their proponents. Ideas cannot be 'owned' by any individual, merely articulated with greater or lesser degrees of success. An argument stands or falls on its own merits.

Offence

Every human interaction carries the potential to cause offence. There are almost no words that are bereft of connotations, and even silence can be a source of discomfort. We can all therefore agree that to insulate ourselves from the possibility of feeling offended is to withdraw from society altogether.

To a degree, it is healthy to shield ourselves from those who would wish to hurt us. We do this in our choice of friends and associates, and on social media this can be accomplished simply by 'blocking' aggressors. An important aspect of freedom of speech is the right not to listen. To claim that using the block function on social media is a form of censorship is akin to saying that one violates Stephen King's free speech by not reading his novels.

But the avoidance of conflict is a tactic that can only ever be effective when it comes to navigating a familiar landscape. In order to live a fulfilling life, we must interact with strangers about whom we know very little. As I have argued, there exists a broadly agreed social contract that protects us from harm, one that is continually subject to revision, but there will always be those who feel compelled, for whatever reason, to transgress the boundaries of acceptable behaviour.

In your adult life, you have taken great care to avoid causing offence wherever possible, but you have not always been successful. This is because our thoughts and intentions are only ever communicated in a partially accurate way. Our choice of language is the most direct means to express what we know ourselves to think and feel, and even then might not best reflect our true sentiments. Even in our moments of greatest clarity, we cannot be certain that our words will be interpreted in the anticipated manner.

When I was a boarding school teacher, one of my charges was a German pupil who had somehow managed to offend every one of his peers. He had developed a reputation for rudeness, and schoolboys are rarely willing to indulge those who are perceived as antagonists. I spoke to the German boy on a number of occasions. Although his English was strong, his utterances would often sound cantankerous or needlessly curt. For instance, rather than say 'Would you mind shutting that door please?' he would say 'You must shut the door now.' As I got to know him better, I soon began to realise that something was being misrepresented in the process of translation. In other words, we were experiencing a version of his personality that was very different from his authentic self.

In a sense, we are all speaking our own unique dialect, even if our language is the same. This is why generosity of interpretation is always to be advised in the first instance. As Socrates observes in Plato's *Meno*, given that misery is the desire and possession of evil, and that nobody desires to be miserable, there can be nobody who knowingly desires evil things. In most cases, it is safest to assume that those who commit acts of which we disapprove must believe them to be good. Similarly, opinions that we find repellent often originate from the best of intentions. Once we understand this, we unlock the potential for meaningful dialogue.

When we are offended, we should think carefully about why we have chosen to take offence and, more importantly, whether or not the offence was meant. In many cases, those who would wish us harm are explicit in their objectives. After all, an expletive-ridden insult is unlikely to be thrown in the spirit of benevolence. But even in such instances, is it right that our personal sensibilities should be the justification for curbing the speech of our traducer?

In part, this is the inevitable corollary of years of risk-averse parenting and teaching strategies, as well as the implementation of anti-bullying measures that have a tendency to catastrophise. As Greg Lukianoff argues, 'People all over the globe are coming to expect emotional and intellectual comfort as though it were a right. This is precisely what you would expect when you train a generation to believe that they have a right not to be offended. Eventually, they stop demanding freedom *of* speech and start demanding freedom *from* speech'. An overdiagnostic culture has reframed distress and emotional pain as forms of mental illness, rather than aspects of a healthy human existence. To feel upset is not an aberration; it is a sign that we are alive.

Let us consider what exactly it means to be offended. There is little doubt that the feeling of offence arises from the disconnect between how things are and how we feel they ought to be. We can be offended by phenomena that do not directly impinge on our lives because they violate our sense of justice. More commonly, we are offended by matters that relate specifically to ourselves. Our pride is injured when we believe that someone holds us in low regard and, as status-seeking primates, we are bound to feel deflated when disparaged.

Once offence has been taken, there are two likely reactions: we might feel that the slight was deserved, and that we should modify our own behaviour in order to avoid similar incidents in the future; alternatively, we might decide that the fault lies with the offender. In these cases, we might seek an apology, retaliate through criticism or mockery, or seek to stop this person from speaking. It is this latter impulse that explains the appeal of censorship as a means to safeguard the feelings of ourselves and others.

To recognise that there are aspects of existence that offend us is not to suggest that the feeling of offence is meaningless. There is nothing wrong with being offended, and it can often spur us into action when it comes to redressing injustice as we see it. That said, if the source of our offence is a general discomfort that others do not behave or speak in accordance with our own specific values, we are engaging in a kind of solipsism that is best avoided, not least because there is no end to the endeavour. This is the kind of mentality that sees people take umbrage on behalf of others, an increasingly common phenomenon by which speech is judged to be 'offensive' even when there is no evidence of any offence being caused.

A compulsion to change the world around us to suit our personal sensibilities is evinced by the tabloid columnist who calls for a film to be banned, the heckler at the comedy club who is outraged at the topic of the joke, the member of staff at a publishing firm who threatens to strike over a 'problematic' author, the student activist who sets off fire alarms to prevent a visiting speaker from upsetting his peers. We understand the impulse because we all feel it from time to time. However, to make the leap from the natural revulsion we experience at certain alternative worldviews to actively silencing them is to surrender to the authoritarian tendency. By doing so, we degrade ourselves by subordinating our reason to baser instincts.

A Thought Experiment

Let us take the specific instance of a visiting speaker at a university campus. Let us suppose that the speaker is a fundamentalist Christian who opposes gay marriage. A group of student activists have threatened to protest in such a way that the security costs have become prohibitive and the speaker is subsequently disinvited.

Although I disapprove of this course of action, I understand the strength of feeling behind it. The students believe that there is no debate still to be had about same-sex marriage, and that to suggest otherwise is to demean gay members of the university community. By prohibiting the speaker from expressing his point of view, gay students can be protected from needless anxiety and harm. Moreover, the success of the protest sends a clear message that the campus is a progressive and inclusive place to live and work.

There are a number of assumptions taking place here all at once. The first is that there is no longer any worthwhile discussion to be had over this subject, although we know from polling that a substantial minority remain unpersuaded of the validity of gay marriage. This isn't equivalent to hosting a debate about whether or not slavery is morally acceptable, a crude comparison which is nonetheless often made. Nobody would think to hold such a debate now, because the matter was resolved in the nineteenth century. The issue of gay rights, on the other hand, has developed comparatively recently and with unprecedented speed. If those who support equal marriage are, as they claim to be, 'on the right side of history', they have nothing to fear from patience.

The range of opinions that are deemed societally acceptable at any given moment is known as the 'Overton Window', and its tendency to shift according to time and location should tell us something about the cultural specificity of ethical norms. There are those who would like to see the Overton Window narrowed to the dimensions of a porthole, with the remaining space conveniently accommodating their own prejudices. When we encounter views that we find intolerable, our instinct nudges us towards enmity. It would make more sense to feel reassured; in a free society, the ocean of competing interests is forever turbulent, and to be offended, therefore, is a sign that ideas are being openly exchanged and not confined to adumbral nooks where they can fester and multiply.

Besides, nobody has ever been persuaded out of a deeply held conviction by force. Gay rights and respectability were not secured by criminalising people who used obsolete and offensive language, or ensuring that those who failed to adapt to changing mores were deprived of a livelihood and publicly shamed. This is the mistake made by those who indulge in cancel culture, most notably the more extreme trans activists whose tactics have generated so much resentment in recent years and, arguably, have done more harm than good for their cause.

We are not fixed in our convictions, and there is certainly more choice involved in our belief systems than we are often prepared to admit. As William Hazlitt said, 'Generally speaking, people stick to an opinion that they have long supported and supports them.' But this illusion of mutual support is most effectively destabilised with carrots rather than sticks. From late antiquity to the Ottoman Empire, the practice of forced conversion has only ever succeeded in compelling the faithful to dissemble and keep their true beliefs hidden. One's personal gods and demons are not so readily slain.

Let us return to our imaginary speaker. I have already addressed the fallacy of assuming that the invitation amounts to an automatic ratification of the speaker's views. Even if this were the case, is there not something to be gained from hearing from those whose ideas we find rebarbative? For one thing, in the very act of attempting to justify their positions, irrational beings are quickly unhorsed. Furthermore, it is always fascinating to hear the indefensible defended, and to catch glimpses into a mind whose worldview is alien to our own. It is like reading the autobiography of a reprobate; behind the malice, there is always something human to quicken our empathy.

I am reminded of the opening of *First Principles* (1862) by the sociologist and philosopher Herbert Spencer, in which he suggests that 'when passing judgment on the opinions of others', we should be willing to concede that there is 'a soul of truth in things erroneous'. Without humility, we are prone to misconstruing the fallibilities of others as signifiers of an intrinsic moral deficiency, what the late Rabbi Jonathan Sacks described as a 'pathological dualism' that divides humanity into 'the unimpeachably good' and 'the irredeemably bad'.

Spencer is especially pertinent because of his tacit support of imperialism and racial cleansing. I doubt I could find another living soul who would not baulk at such ideas, but would it really be wise to dismiss Spencer's entire output on this basis? Like all of us, Spencer was a product of his era, and while we are right to condemn notions we now know to be abhorrent, we must also be able to recognise that we would not be so damning in our judgement had we been born into his time and circumstances. It is only by contextualising the failures of the past that we are able to learn from them.

And what of our imaginary protesters? Leaving aside the myriad concerns we might have about a student body for whom emotional safekeeping takes priority over intellectual rigour, their boycotting makes little sense on its own terms. It is clear that the protesters suppose that the public communication of pernicious views will enable them to spread like an airborne virus, and that we would therefore be better off keeping them contained. The history of censorship shows us the folly of this approach, which is why the metaphor of sunlight being the best disinfectant is so commonly heard. Milton envisaged this as a battlefield, with Truth and Falsehood as the antagonists. 'Let her and Falsehood grapple; who ever knew Truth put to the worse, in a free and open encounter?' We are far better placed to know and overcome evil if we are acquainted with its essence, and the best way to achieve this is to listen and to read.

If we grant leeway for bad ideas to go unchallenged, they are able to sustain the illusion of incontrovertibility among their devotees. This has never been more obviously the case than in the age of the Internet. When social media tech giants choose to censor certain topics, they invariably sweep them elsewhere, usually to the uncharted recesses of cyberspace where the light of reason cannot hope to penetrate.

In forcing the disinvitation of a speaker, the protesters have deprived themselves of the chance to prove that their opposition is sound. Even if one could say for certain that the protesters were in the right, unless they are able to explain and defend their view they are merely holding what John Stuart Mill described as 'a dead dogma, not a living truth'. In open debate they might expose the flaws of the speaker's stance and, better still, persuade others of their way of thinking. Furthermore, the stifling of speech can have the unintended consequence of making martyrs out of those who have been silenced and enabling them to portray themselves as oppressed tellers of uncomfortable truths. It has a glamourising effect that, if anything, enhances their appeal.

In addition, it generates resentment among those who have had the decision of whether or not to attend the event taken away from them. The protesters have effectively acted *in loco parentis*, infantilising their peers by judging on their behalf what forms of speech would be hurtful for them to hear. In this, they are often aided by a university administration that would rather avoid negative publicity than defend the principles by which the institution stands or falls. The implication in our imaginary scenario, whether intended or not, is that gay students are compromised by listening to a speaker express disapproval of their lifestyle, and that they are incapable of presenting a counter-argument. Most gay people would rather not be patronised in this way. Nor does it help anyone to pretend that the debate is about gay people's 'right to exist'. Such histrionic straw men have no place in adult discussion.

If the protesters were likely to be offended by the event, they could simply have opted not to attend. If they were particularly incensed, they might have organised a peaceful protest to raise awareness of the content of the speaker's address, and let their peers make their own choices. By sitting in judgement on what is best for others, they ultimately weaken their own enterprise.

Perhaps our protesters feel that inviting a speaker who opposes same-sex marriage is the equivalent of bringing a fascist into their midst. The policy of 'No Platforming' originates from the National Union of Students (NUS) conference of April 1974, in which a resolution was passed that would debar 'openly racist or fascist organisations or societies' from speaking on campus. Such measures were understandable at a time when racist groups had a degree of popular support, although as Brendan O'Neill points out, even at the time of its inauguration there were concerns that the policy was likely to expand and had the 'potential to generate other targets for censorship'.

Now that racist and fascist groups are universally despised in civilised society, the prohibition only makes sense if we artificially expand the definitions of these terms to incorporate anyone whose ideas fail to live up to contemporary values, particularly in relation to modern-day 'social justice'. This is known as 'concept creep', and it explains why words such as 'racist' and 'fascist' are now so promiscuously applied.

There is considerable evidence of the ways in which various terms – e.g., 'fascist', 'Nazi', 'racist', 'homophobe', 'transphobe', 'misogynist' – have become so nebulous that their potency has been irredeemably reduced. This not only provides shelter for the very people such words would accurately describe, it also hinders our efforts to identify them in a meaningful way. Thanks to years of concept creep, whenever I come across any of these terms on social media, in mainstream news outlets, or in the language of politicians, my initial instinct is to assume that the epithet has been misused. The boy has cried 'fascist' once too often, and is now being ignored.

It is a great irony that the strategy of smearing people as racist without cause is only successful because we live in a country that no longer considers racism in any way valid. Even the allegation is sufficient to make the accused unemployable. In other words, the charge that ours is an endemically racist culture is fatally undermined by the very tactics that its proponents deploy. They prove that our society is committed to expelling the very racism they claim defines it.

In truth, these phrases have become catch-alls for *personae non gratae*. By branding people in this way, our protesters feel disobliged from rebutting their views, or even treating them with basic human courtesy. Our imaginary speaker opposes same-sex marriage, and can therefore be monstered as a homophobe and a fascist. Even his choice of phrasing – 'same-sex marriage' rather than 'equal marriage' – marks him out as an antediluvian relic whose views do not merit the attention of those who know better. Yet thirty years ago his view would have been the prevailing one, and those who might have endorsed the now mainstream opinion would have been left stranded outside of the Overton Window.

Progress is only ever made when the dissenters are heard. 'If liberty means anything at all', wrote Orwell, 'it means the right to tell people what they do not want to hear.' This is not to suggest that all forms of dissent are inherently progressive, but if we only ever expose ourselves to the received wisdom of the present, we condemn ourselves to eternal stasis.

Comedy and Satire

As the boundaries of social acceptability shift this way and that depending on the cultural mores of any given time, comedians will reliably be found capering along the perimeter. Like Lear's fool, they are licensed to speak truth to power and keep their heads. They test the limits of our tolerance, give voice to the taboos of our age, and play with social decorum like a cat with a cornered mouse. Sometimes, the mouse gets eaten.

A few years ago, I gave a talk on comedy and satire at a school in London. At one point, I asked the pupils to raise their hands if they felt that there should be legal limits on what comedians are permitted to joke about. The majority of hands went up, something that would have been inconceivable when I was at school. The pupils were open-minded and were able to reflect on whether this was a sign of progress or back-pedalling to the illiberal trends of the past, but this generational divide was a reminder of how freedom of speech is eroded if not continually defended over time.

Comedy cannot exist without the possibility of causing offence. We should not be surprised, therefore, to see that comedians are regularly in the news for taking a joke 'too far'. Satirists are particularly likely to transgress the limits of acceptable discourse, because their goal is to expose the vices and follies of the powerful. The history books are littered with the corpses of satirists who have tickled a few too many delicate nerves. On tarot cards, the fool is depicted as singing or playing a pipe as, quite oblivious to the danger, he skips off the edge of a precipice.

Stéphane Charbonnier (known as 'Charb'), cartoonist and editor-in-chief of the French satirical magazine *Charlie Hebdo*, was once asked whether he feared reprisals after he published cartoons of the Prophet Mohammed. In his answer, he paraphrased the Mexican revolutionary Emiliano Zapata: 'I would rather die standing than live on my knees.' A little over two years later, he was killed along with eleven others in the Islamist terror attack on the *Charlie Hebdo* offices.

The shockwaves from this tragedy are still reverberating. In October 2020, schoolteacher Samuel Paty was beheaded by a terrorist in Paris for showing images from *Charlie Hebdo* in a lesson about free speech. There followed a series of murders by Islamic fundamentalists, and many commentators and politicians began to question whether the French constitutional fealty to the principle of *laïcité* was the problem. The *Associated Press* asked, 'Why does France incite anger in the Muslim world?' claiming that the country was targeted for its 'brutal colonial past, staunch secular policies and tough-talking president who is seen as insensitive toward the Muslim faith'. *Politico* followed suit, attacking 'France's dangerous religion of secularism'. The Canadian prime minister Justin Trudeau claimed that 'freedom of expression is not without limits. We owe it to ourselves to act with respect for others and to seek not to arbitrarily or unnecessarily injure those with whom we are sharing a society and a planet.' Like the massacre at *Charlie Hebdo*, condolences in the aftermath were tainted by a lingering sense that the victims were to blame, and that by expressing themselves a little too freely they had forfeited their freedom to exist.

Few passions are quite so intense as religious devotion, and it is unsurprising that many Muslims would feel distress at seeing their prophet caricatured. This explains why the likes of Trudeau are in favour of limiting speech to protect certain groups from being lampooned. However, as I have already noted, defining such parameters is a Sisyphean task, and the natural and ineluctable human tendency to take offence makes it impossible to legislate against its possibility. Furthermore, as Charb noted in an 'open letter' completed just two days before his death, the idea that a non-believer is capable of blasphemy is incoherent. 'God is only sacred to those who believe in him,' he wrote. 'If you wish to insult or offend God, you have to be sure that he exists.'

A misleading narrative has dominated discussions of the *Charlie Hebdo* atrocity, one that is largely based on the false impression that the magazine routinely 'punches down' at minority ethnic groups. As Robert McLiam Wilson has pointed out, the majority of *Charlie Hebdo*'s critics have a number of shared qualities: they are not regular readers of the magazine; they live outside of France; and they don't speak French. This explains why the depiction of justice minister Christiane Taubira as a monkey was so widely interpreted as racist, even though the target was the racist nationalists who had made such appalling comparisons in the first place. There is a very good reason why this left-wing magazine has been lauded as 'the greatest anti-racist weekly' by SOS Racisme, a group well known for its campaigns against racial discrimination.

Moreover, *Charlie Hebdo* forms part of a longstanding pedigree of abrasive and offensive satirical cartooning which includes publications such as *La Caricature* (1830–43), *Le Rire* (1894–1971), *Le Sourire de France* (1899–1940) and *L'Assiette au Beurre* (1901–12). This tradition has its origins in the early 1830s, when the caricaturist Charles Philipon was repeatedly jailed for drawing King Louis Philippe as a pear.

In all satirical traditions, authority is the target, whether that takes the form of kings reduced to the status of fruit, or ideological figureheads reconceptualised in sexually compromising scenarios. *Charlie Hebdo*'s depictions of Mohammed – like its cartoon of the Holy Trinity, in which the Son, the Father and the Holy Spirit are seen engaged in a three-way sexual encounter – are not 'punching down' at ordinary Muslims, but 'punching up' at the icons of powerful global religions. After all, you can't punch much higher than God.

Even if we could find irrefutable proof that the magazine's consistent track record of opposing racism – including support for further legal protections for ethnic minorities and voting rights for immigrants – was a front for far-right sympathies, demands for censorship would still constitute an infringement on artistic freedom. Yet the fact that so many believe that the state should constrain the cartoonists of *Charlie Hebdo* reveals the danger of the very concept of hate speech laws. That is to say, if a substantial number of intelligent people can become convinced that a left-wing anti-racist publication is waging a war against minority ethnic groups, then it is surely inevitable that legislation against 'hate' will be enforced on the basis of similar misconceptions.

For the atheist satirists of *Charlie Hebdo*, religion is an ideology like any other and has no right to be cushioned from derision. As Charb put it: 'While, unlike the existence of God, it is difficult to deny the existence of Marx, Lenin or Georges Marchais, it is neither blasphemous, racist nor communistophobic to cast doubt on the validity of their writings or their speech. In France, a religion is nothing more than a collection of texts, traditions and customs that it is perfectly legitimate to criticise. Sticking a clown nose on Marx is no more offensive or scandalous than popping the same schnoz on Muhammad.'

For devout believers, Islamic prohibitions against pictorial representations of their prophet only exacerbate the sense of grievance, which is why so many find this comparison unconvincing. But in order to criticise *Charlie Hebdo*, as is anyone's right, one must first understand the subject of one's criticism. To excoriate these cartoonists for racism is to lock horns with a phantom enemy. If satirists are to self-censor due to the possibility of misinterpretation, we may as well abandon the genre altogether.

The Self-Censoring
Artist

———

Amid the rabble of tourists that typically undulate in and around Florence's Piazza della Signoria, you would be forgiven for heedlessly stepping over the round marble plaque that marks the spot where the Dominican Friar Girolamo Savonarola was hanged and incinerated in 1498. His fate had a certain talionic quality, for only a year before, in this same square, his followers had orchestrated their famous 'bonfire of the vanities'. In a frenzy of religious fervour, they had torched thousands of objects associated with sin and moral degeneracy: cosmetics, dresses, mirrors, perfumes, books and even musical instruments. The city had been spellbound by Savonarola's fanaticism, and were purging themselves before the apocalypse that their new spiritual leader insisted was imminent. It is said that Sandro Botticelli cast a number of his own paintings on to the pyre, and it is difficult to conceive a more evocative image of artistic self-censorship. If the story is true, we may have lost significant works of art because their creator had allowed a doom-mongering monk to throttle his muse.

Artists of today may not be throwing their work on to bonfires in order to appease the wrath of God, but they are still under pressure from ideologues to self-censor. Writers and comedians in particular have grown cautious about producing potentially sensitive material, and to be seen to align with the views of the creative industries' many gatekeepers. Critics, too, now regularly assess artistic works on the basis of how closely the artist reflects their own ideological perspective. It goes without saying that total objectivity is neither possible nor desirable when it comes to professional criticism, but it would appear that a significant proportion now see their role as censuring art that they perceive to be 'problematic'.

Moral responsibility is the albatross around the artist's neck. Those who are preoccupied with how their work might be misinterpreted, or how it might influence the behaviour of its audience, are wont to stumble into the trap of didacticism. Definitions of 'art' are rarely satisfactory, but I'll settle for Émile Zola's description of art as 'life seen through a temperament'. That is not to suggest that great art cannot be political or pedagogic, but it invariably suffers when the artist is compelled in this direction against his or her will. It is likewise detrimental to our enjoyment of art if we are obliged to react from a position of rectitude. It is perfectly legitimate to appreciate a work of art while detesting its underlying moral intention.

When we think of censorship our minds run to the draconianism of the Star Chamber, the Bishops' Ban of 1599, the *Index Librorum Prohibitorum* of the Catholic Inquisition, or the burning of books in Nazi Germany. But self-censorship can be just as damaging to the artistic health of a nation. The explosion of social media has provided a forum in which non-conformist viewpoints can be lambasted in the most public way, with artistic representation being continually scrutinised through the lens of identity politics. Under such circumstances, self-censorship is the probable outcome. Artists are intrinsically deviant; they revel in artifice and fantasy, twisting the landscape to their own whims. Conformity is their oubliette.

We can all agree that the censorship of artists by tyrannous regimes is an abomination, and yet there is something even more dispiriting about an artist who surrenders his or her freedom of expression voluntarily. In its most extreme form, self-censorship occurs because of the prospect of violent repercussions. For most artists, however, the threat they face is that of limited career prospects in a risk-averse climate. Work that is genuinely controversial invariably faces a barrage of voluble criticism online. Of course, there is nothing new in this – every age has its puritans – only now those in powerful positions in the creative industries tend to appease the tantrums of those who scream the loudest.

Once artists begin tailoring their work in accordance with how they sense it will be received, their craft is bound to deteriorate. The novelist Forrest Reid observed that the writer could choose one of two incompatible aims: 'He may look upon his work as an art to be practised with sincerity, and in faithfulness to an ideal; or he may regard it as a commercial experiment.' For those whose goal is to make money and acquire fame, adherence to what Mill described as the 'despotism of custom' is nothing to fear. For the true artist, such obsequiousness is a kind of death.

The practical demands of human existence can be something of a distraction from the artist's vocation. This is why some of the most prolific have come from independently wealthy backgrounds. In his essay 'The Soul of Man Under Socialism', Oscar Wilde argued that individuality can only flourish in times of leisure. The Ancient Greeks were able to develop great philosophy, art and literature because, disgracefully, they had slaves to take care of all the menial tasks that occupy most people's lives. Poets and writers enjoyed a Renaissance in Britain in the sixteenth century because of aristocratic patronage. With arts funding today largely reserved for those who can prove that their work entails some practical benefit to society, artists face growing pressure to ensure that they are commercially viable.

Of course, it is not in the nature of artists to admit that they are curtailing their own manner of expression in the face of external influences, which means that the problem is likely to be more widespread than we imagine. The best artists are non-conformists, and the worst artists like to be seen as the best artists. We should do all we can to cultivate a world in which creative risks are worth taking, and in which eccentricity and missteps will not be punished in the kangaroo courts of social media.

An artist who kowtows to ideological expectations can barely be said to be an artist at all. Like RS Thomas's toiling farmer, he is merely 'contributing grimly to the accepted pattern, the embryo music dead in his throat'.

The New Conformity

The implications for self-censorship are as troubling for the general population as they are for artists. When George Orwell wrote his essay on 'The English People' in 1944, he was able to assert that extremely few 'are afraid to utter their political opinions in public, and there are not even very many who want to silence the opinions of others'. This sentence could not be written with any confidence today.

The phenomenon of 'shy voters', as evinced by wildly inaccurate opinion polls in both the United Kingdom's European Union referendum of 2016 and the United States elections of 2016 and 2020, is an example of what the economist Timur Kuran has called 'preference falsification', whereby one's true opinions are withheld in favour of more socially acceptable alternatives. When our elected representatives fall prey to this tendency it makes a sham of political discourse, reducing it to a pantomime of heroes and villains.

Preference falsification is not exclusive to politics. As moral norms shift, and the opinions of yesterday become not only unfashionable but proscribed, our willingness to share our authentic feelings is inhibited. William Hazlitt had this in mind when he said that 'if you set your face against custom, people will set their faces against you'. As social creatures, our fear of unpopularity is innate, yet to repress the truth is to leave unchecked a parasite gnawing at the soul. We make ourselves vulnerable because we are colluding with those we have deceived in what amounts to an artificial reality. The pressure to lie corrals us into a morally compromising position where, for the sake of our sanity, we learn to believe our own fictions, condemned to live as actors who have forgotten we are playing a role.

More often than not, preference falsification is the symptom of the desire for an easy life. Conflict is hard. The appeal of ideologies is that they absolve us of the obligation to think for ourselves. Many, if not most, are willing to sacrifice their freedom of speech and independent thought for the consolations of certitude. It is in the interests of the powerful to encourage this kind of docility and thereby beget a flock of industrious sheep.

Whatever the motive – desire to be liked, fear of animosity, submission to authority for the stability it brings – we find that in many cases the greatest threat to free expression comes from ourselves. In *On Liberty* (1859), John Stuart Mill repeatedly emphasises the danger of outsourcing our moral agency to the putative wisdom of the crowd. Mill understood that our freedom of speech is not imperilled solely by the state's abuse of power, but also by what he describes as 'the tyranny of the prevailing opinion and feeling'. His treatise is a cogent vindication of the primacy of the individual.

The implications for higher education are especially dire. Historically, attacks on academic freedom have come from external political forces. One thinks of how intellectuals were consigned to labour camps during the Chinese Cultural Revolution, or the present-day Turkish Government's incursions against the institutions of higher education. In modern liberal democracies, the most pressing threats arise within the system itself. Largely, this is down to lack of viewpoint diversity among teaching staff; according to one study, less than 12 per cent of academic staff are right-leaning, as compared to roughly half of the national population. The expectation to conform to a particular political and ideological worldview has encouraged many academics to self-censor and circumscribed the career prospects of those who do not. A 2020 report found that one in three conservative scholars claim to self-censor 'for fear of consequences to [their] career'.

Pressure has also come from the students themselves. A 2017 study by the Foundation for Individual Rights in Education (FIRE) revealed that a majority of students feel that 'it is important to be part of a campus community where they are not exposed to intolerant or offensive ideas'. Sometimes, these demands for protection have escalated into acts of outright intimidation. In November 2015, Erika Christakis, a lecturer at Yale University, emailed the student body to question the wisdom of a proposed ban on offensive Hallowe'en costumes. In response, students gathered outside her home and wrote various menacing statements in chalk such as: 'We know where you live'.

When the master of the college Nicholas Christakis, husband to Erika, agreed to meet them in the courtyard, he was surrounded, verbally abused and even instructed not to smile or make any gestures. A video of the confrontation went viral in which one young woman is seen screaming directly at Christakis,

'You should step down! It is not about creating an intellectual space! It is not! Do you understand that? It's about creating a home here. You are not doing that!' A year later, Erika Christakis wrote of the support she and her husband had received via private correspondence, but noted that colleagues were too frightened to risk defending them in public.

The case of Evergreen State College in Olympia, Washington, is equally disturbing. In 2017, a change had been made to the college's annual 'Day of Absence' protest, in which ethnic minority students had the choice to remove themselves from the campus in order to highlight the importance of their contri- bution to university life. This year it was decided that white students and staff should leave the premises instead. A biology professor, Bret Weinstein, objected to the notion of compulsory absence on the basis of skin colour. His refusal to acquiesce to the demands of the protesters, and his determination not to apologise, led to days of unrest during which time the students took over the university, occupying and barricading the admin- istration building and effectively holding members of staff hostage for hours.

With students demanding intellectual 'safety', occasionally in the most bellicose and intimidating manner, it is not surpris- ing that academics have learned to be reticent when it comes to expressing views that deviate from the norm. The costs to the intellectual wellbeing of society can hardly be overestimated. Just as great art flourishes where eccentricity is tolerated, aca- demic innovation depends upon those who do not conform to received wisdom, or at the very least are willing to see it tested.

Mill asserted that 'the amount of eccentricity in a society has generally been proportional to the amount of genius, mental vigour, and moral courage it contained'. An academic environment in which non-conformist viewpoints are mistrusted is a virtual guarantee of stultification. As Joanna Williams argues in her book *Academic Freedom in an Age of Conformity* (2016), 'personal freedom is a prerequisite for both a critique of conventional knowledge and the search for the new'.

Self-censorship is not to be confused with choosing our words with diligence, which is the duty of anyone who wishes to participate in civilised society. This was the key idea behind the 'political correctness' movement of the late 1980s and early 1990s, which, for all its miscalculations and occasional lapses into zealotry, helped to cultivate a consensus on politeness. The sledgehammer tactics of contemporary cancel culture have little to do with political correctness as traditionally understood. Tacit social contracts concerning polite speech in the workplace, schools or public spaces are hardly a controversial notion. We all adhere to such principles in one form or another, albeit with some inevitable sticking points and disagreements along the way. Cancel culture is a mutated form of political correctness that seeks to police language and thought alike. It is a type of soft authoritarianism that accentuates the problems of division and intolerance as it attempts to mitigate their effects.

It is to the advantage of those who wish to deny cancel culture to conflate the political correctness movement of the late twentieth century with the problems we face today. It enables them to caricature the debate in tabloid terms – 'PC' versus 'non-PC' or 'snowflake' versus 'anti-snowflake' – whereas, in reality, it is closer to Mill's conception of the 'struggle between Liberty and Authority'. These are the two narratives of what has become known as today's 'culture war', one a cartoonish misrepresentation, the other a sincere effort to uphold the lynchpins of democracy. We should be wary, then, of those who dismiss legitimate criticisms of cancel culture and state over-reach as the paranoid wittering of the 'PC-gone-mad brigade'. This is merely a form of tactical prestidigitation which under-mines the serious business of defending our freedoms.

Self-censorship, then, is not just a matter of holding back on expressing ourselves out of fear that we might be attacked for our candour, or unfairly stigmatised for holding contentious views. It is the inescapable product of a climate in which discus-sion of sensitive topics has become potentially career-ending with little possibility of redemption.

Ultimately, however, self-censorship is a choice, even at a time when speaking out can have ruinous personal consequences. Conformity and dishonesty for the sake of self-preservation are understandable, but are an affront to our conscience and dignity. We might avoid the ire of the bullies in the short term, but the eventual impact of our collective silence will be an enervated and infantile culture.

Persuasion and Debate

Language is powerful. Ever since antiquity, the greatest thinkers have understood that even good ideas are worthless if argued badly. From the late medieval period, students at Oxford and Cambridge were first taught the *trivium* of grammar, logic and rhetoric. The last is best defined as 'the art of persuasion', a tradition that harks back to the Attic orators of Ancient Greece, and the works of Cicero during the Roman Republic. The most memorable political speeches of recent history, from the Gettysburg Address (1863) to Martin Luther King's 'I have a dream' (1963), have built upon this cultural inheritance.

Shakespeare likewise appreciated that an inability to persuade is the harbinger of failure. It is Coriolanus's arrogant belief that he need not win the approval of the plebeians that guarantees his eventual downfall. By contrast, Mark Antony manages to turn a crowd against Julius Caesar's assassins in fewer than a hundred lines. In the case of Lady Macbeth, we see how finely wrought rhetoric can be exploited to viperous ends.

She is able to drive her husband to commit regicide through some elegantly crafted slurs against his masculinity.

We are all susceptible to influence, and that is a positive sign. It means that most of us are keeping an open mind. The downside is that we may be seduced into courses of action that are harmful to either ourselves or others. It goes without saying that language is the key to manipulation. Who would deny that the rise of Nazism was accelerated by Hitler's fluency and oratorical skills?

With the advantage of hindsight, it is easy to claim that, had Hitler been silenced, the tragedy of the Second World War might have been averted. We forget, however, that attempts to do just that sometimes led to the amplification of his message. Prominent Nazis such as Joseph Goebbels and Theodor Fritsch were prosecuted for their anti-Semitism under the hate speech laws of the Weimar Republic. Julius Streicher, the man responsible for the anti-Semitic newspaper *Der Stürmer*, was twice imprisoned and his publication repeatedly confiscated by the authorities. As Flemming Rose has pointed out, each time the editors were taken to court, the cases 'served as effective public-relations machinery, affording Streicher the kind of attention he would never have found in a climate of a free and open debate'.

If hate speech laws failed to impede the spread of evil ideas during the years preceding the Third Reich, is it likely that they would be more effective elsewhere? Moreover, which figures of authority do we trust to decide which ideas are evil and which are good? In the United Kingdom, hate speech laws as encapsulated in the Public Order Act 1986 and the Communications Act 2003 have led to investigations, arrests and prosecutions for insults, contentious opinions and even jokes. These cases serve as a reminder that the state is not to be trusted with the authority to impede speech.

Even if you maintain that occasional abuses of state power are a small price to pay for healthy public discourse, I would ask you to consider the inherent dangers of this precedent. Milton offers the example of the Spanish Inquisition, and how their acts of censorship, although ostensibly intended to purge the world of heresy, soon came to include 'any subject that was not to their palate'. When it comes to defining what constitutes unacceptable speech, the notion of true objectivity is a mirage.

This is especially concerning in a climate in which, as we have seen, even terms such as 'fascist' have become unmoored from their original definitions. If the Government were to limit the application of hate speech laws to fascists, we would still be left with the problem that most people currently branded as such are nothing of the kind. When mainstream journalists are claiming that 'fascism is being normalised', and politicians are referring to Brexit as a 'fascist coup', how can we be sure that our government will not pivot into similarly hyperbolic territory?

Plenty of activists support this view that fascism has now been 'normalised' in our society, in spite of evidence that it has been in terminal decline for decades. Through discussion, the reality might be better understood, but this is precisely the kind of discussion that many on the left refuse to dignify with their participation. By their reasoning, to debate those whose ideology has already been roundly quashed would be to prop up a corpse that we would all rather leave to decompose.

Herein lies the contradiction: either fascism has been defeated and lies in ruins at the fringes of society, or it is a major threat that is growing day by day. Either it is a marginal view that we can safely ignore because all civilised people oppose it, or its disciples are rapidly insinuating themselves into the body politic. If the latter is true, and it has indeed regained mass appeal, then exposing it through debate becomes a matter of obligation. If it is false, then we should not be elevating the significance of the far right by asserting that they enjoy a degree of support far in excess of the reality. To do so is merely to act in the interests of those we oppose.

In truth, there is broad consensus about the futility of debating long-defeated ideas, which is why teachers of History do not introduce their pupils to Holocaust denial as an alternative theory for the sake of 'balance'. But with the concept creep I have described, important conversations are stifled before they can even begin. For example, when so-called 'TERFs' (Trans Exclusionary Radical Feminists) are casually stigmatised as 'fascists' and 'bigots', and No Platformed on that basis, there can be no possibility of mutual understanding between conflicting groups. I would no more debate a fascist than I would a madman; that is a task for experts in deradicalisation. However, I would happily debate an individual who has profound concerns about the economic impact of mass immigration, even if he has been unfairly branded a 'fascist' by the historically illiterate.

Where nobody can agree on definitions, there can be no unanimity on where the limitations of free speech can be drawn. In such circumstances, the safest approach is to defend free speech for all, and that includes those whose views we might find reprehensible.

Words and Violence

'When the conversation ceases,' says Daryl Davis, 'the ground will become fertile for violence,' Freedom of speech does not guarantee that violent people will be redeemed, but it does at least mean that the possibility is not precluded. As Tony Benn said, 'All war represents a failure of diplomacy.' Recourse to violence is often a desperate measure of those who feel unheard. While this should not be taken to mean that bloodshed ought to be justified, it is a reminder that the stifling of speech can have disastrous consequences.

But what happens when the difference between words and violence is no longer recognised? On 20 March 2017, six professors at Wellesley College in Massachusetts sent a group email to colleagues advising them to refrain from inviting potentially controversial speakers to the campus for fear of causing offence. Faculty members were encouraged to make no distinction between words and physical violence. The professors discussed a disturbing 'pattern of harm' in the speakers thus far invited. They described how students had been left 'in distress' at having to listen to such 'painful' ideas. These talks had caused 'damage', and any who had had the courage to rebut the speakers' arguments had experienced 'injury' as a result.

The beginning of this trend can probably be traced to what Greg Lukianoff and Jonathan Haidt have described as a new culture of 'Safetyism', one that has emerged partly thanks to overprotective parents who wish to shield their offspring from all conceivable risk, but also due to the cultivation of 'safe spaces' on university campuses. The result has been a reconceptualisation of what it means to be 'safe', which elides emotional and physical harm. Similarly, subjective experience has become 'definitional in assessing trauma' in the therapeutic community, which means that anything that causes emotional distress can be deemed traumatic.

The conflation of words and violence, so common among those who support No Platforming and cancel culture more generally, can often feel like rhetorical sleight of hand, or a kind of emotional blackmail. A more generous interpretation is offered by psychologist Lisa Feldman Barrett: 'If words can cause stress,' she writes, 'and if prolonged stress can cause physical harm, then it seems that speech – at least certain types of speech – can be a form of violence.' Yet the logic of this reasoning would see all potential sources of stress as tantamount to violence, which could apply to just about anything. If I become anxious due to financial problems brought about by taxes on my income, and fall ill as a result, has the Government committed an act of violence against my person by means of taxation? Surely even the staunchest libertarian would regard this as wishful thinking.

I have some sympathy with Barrett's reasoning, not least because I am naturally concerned about the immense stress that those who are verbally abused can suffer. But insults are not threats, and there is something undeniably opportunistic about invoking 'safety' as a tactic to prevent others from speaking. It has the effect of destabilising the terms of debate, reimagining two opposing points of view as a struggle between the oppressor and the oppressed, the violent and the victimised. While it is conceivable that an individual might feel anxiety upon being challenged, this does not invalidate the challenge itself or necessarily prove that it is malignant in intent. By reframing certain opinions as violence, activists are able to justify censorship as a form of self-defence, thereby exempting themselves from ever having to validate their own arguments or engage with those of others.

We have seen this recently with the conflict between those who support gender self-identification and feminists who are worried about single-sex spaces being open to those who identify as female but are anatomically male. A vocal minority of trans activists have branded anyone who expresses such concerns as 'transphobic', and claimed that they are striving to 'erase the existence of trans people'. The alarmist turn of phrase might well be felt sincerely in some cases, but is more often an example of strategic hyperbole of a similar kind to the accusation that words 'do harm' and 'threaten safety'.

This insistence that words can be a form of violence, that ideas cause injury or erase one's existence, has a further, more sinister, effect. It means that inflicting physical harm on one's ideological opponents can be excused as a form of self-defence. Lukianoff and Haidt have cited studies that show that a substantial proportion of the student population believe that acts of physical violence are 'acceptable' when used against those with 'hateful views'. When alt-right figurehead Richard Spencer was punched during an interview in Washington, many were quick to support his assailant. The *Guardian* published an extended piece of sophistry on the subject of whether or not it was ethical to punch a Nazi.

The danger of this reasoning should be obvious. Nobody is suggesting that we have a responsibility to seek out neo-Nazi thugs or Ku Klux Klan members and debate them, but surrendering the moral high ground to the likes of Spencer can hardly be said to be a shrewd move. As Hannah Arendt observed, political violence is inherently self-defeating because 'the means used to achieve political goals are more often than not of greater relevance to the future world than the intended goals'. However justifiable or rational our objectives might be, recourse to violence has a delegitimising effect, and its inherent 'arbitrariness' is likely to result in increasingly unpredictable cycles of conflict.

Liberalism offers a social contract by which we are entitled to attack people verbally so long as we cede the right to do so physically. As Adam Gopnik points out, 'an assault on an ideology is not merely different from a threat made to a person; it is the opposite of a threat made to a person'. When we interpret violence as speech or speech as violence we are disrupting the conditions by which the social contract can function. There is a world of difference between barbed words and barbed wire.

Identity Quakes

It is somewhat inevitable that language and, by extension, freedom of speech, should come to be mistrusted given that most of these recent developments are connected to the rise of an identity-orientated social justice ideology which is largely postmodernist in origin. In particular, contemporary activists have retained the postmodernist notion that reality, or at least our perception of it, is constructed predominantly through language. Michel Foucault's belief in the interconnectivity of power and knowledge is often seen as the basis for current discourses of the 'power structures' that dominate society. In this model, language is not only a means of communication, but a weapon of the powerful to maintain their hegemony. This is why those who support censorship often claim that unfettered speech has the effect of 'normalising' or 'legitimising' hateful and violent views. As I have outlined, this does not merely apply to insulting or offensive sentiments, but also transgressive opinions.

We have all felt that sensation of disquietude when our most cherished certainties are challenged. Tom Holland has noted how the palaeontologist Edward Drinker Cope, who was raised a Quaker and taught that the Bible was the literal truth, was 'so unsettled by the dinosaurs he found entombed in rock that they came to visit him in his dreams', where they would kick and trample upon him. A similar crisis of faith befell Charles Darwin, who could not reconcile the notion of a 'beneficent and omnipotent God' with the brutal reproductive practices of the ichneumon wasp, which paralyses caterpillars with its sting so that its larvae can develop inside a living host. Darwin's Christian identity was shaken by the evident cruelty of the natural world.

Such realisations are known as 'identity quakes', described by Peter Boghossian and James Lindsay as the 'emotional reaction that follows from having one's core values disrupted'. For the open-minded, life is by necessity punctuated with these little shocks of awakening. Without introspection, there can be no individual development. We all remember Socrates's famous dictum that the unexamined life is not worth living, and it seems to me that we deny ourselves the opportunity for growth when we refuse to interrogate our own certainties. It is intellectual suicide in slow motion.

Words are indubitably a potential source of great distress, whether that takes the form of a challenge to our worldview or outright abuse. Yet taking offence is a matter of choice. Marcus Aurelius said it this way: 'Choose not to be harmed – and you won't feel harmed. Don't feel harmed – and you haven't been'. Of course, we have every reason to suppose that the life of a Roman emperor might be more comfortable than ours but, in the interests of self-preservation, there is something to be said for the stoical ethos.

It comes down to a question of consent. If a man were to punch me, or otherwise inflict harm upon me by physical means, I am in no position to prevent the injury. There is no such loss of liberty in the taking of offence, which has come about as a combination of the words uttered and the interpretation or significance I place upon them. This is why the law is right to prohibit physical assault but permit the casting of insults. In the case of the former, the incursion on my liberties justifies my recourse to see my offender prosecuted; the attack satisfied his will at the expense of mine. The same cannot be said were I to attempt to silence my critic, in which case I would be the one guilty of encroaching on the liberty of another.

The fear of emotional pain can be crippling, and the desire to protect ourselves from it is as natural as our instinct to withdraw from fire. While I am not sufficiently pessimistic to subscribe to Thomas Hardy's notion of happiness as 'the occasional episode in a general drama of pain' – probably the most depressing final sentence of a novel ever penned – a healthy recognition of life's difficulties is surely the most effective method of insulating ourselves from chaos.

Incitement

Once we have reinstated this distinction between words and violence, we might then move on to consider the question of how the one can lead to the other. This is perhaps the most compelling argument for restrictions on speech. If it can be determined that certain forms of speech incite violence, then there is a case to be made that responsibility is thereby shared between the perpetrator of the crime and the individual who provoked it.

The Rwandan genocide of 1994 is frequently cited in order to demonstrate a causal relationship between speech and violence. The RTLM radio broadcasts that called on Hutus to 'cut down the tall trees' and described the Tutsi minority as 'cockroaches' and 'snakes' – dehumanising language reminiscent of the Nazi propaganda that depicted Jews as rats – are said to be culpable in the stirring up of a maelstrom of hatred that resulted in the murder of almost a million people.

Incitement to violence has always been an offence under English common law, but the definition has also been open to subjective interpretation. At what point might we claim that a criminal's individual responsibility is shared by those who inspired it, and how is this to be quantified? There is no human act that could not be said to have been prompted to a degree by some external influence, and there is no penalty for a criminal that might not be mitigated through appeal to extenuating circumstances outlined by a honey-tongued defence lawyer. This is why so many find the notion of personal responsibility intuitively reasonable; it has the effect of tidying up an otherwise messy business.

Yet these are complicated matters that are unlikely to be resolved with binary thinking. If we as a society wish to legislate against speech that has the potential to incite violence, we need to consider how such influences can be proven and to what extent they exist at all. After Brenda Spencer went on a shooting spree at the Grover Cleveland Elementary School in 1979, she reportedly explained her actions by saying, 'I don't like Mondays.' If we were to take this on trust, would there be a case for outlawing Mondays on the grounds that the day incites violence?

This may seem flippant, but the principle stands. In the history of human conflict – which is to say the history of humanity – there have been no intentional acts of violence bereft of impetus. These are as varied as the imagination will allow: an alarming report on the evening news; a misspoken word from a family member; an overheard conversation in a pub. You can be sure that any conceivable phenomenon has, at some point or other, triggered a reaction in those predisposed to act violently.

In the wake of the terrorist atrocity in New Zealand in March 2019 – in which a far-right terrorist murdered fifty-one Muslim worshippers and injured another forty – angry students accosted Chelsea Clinton, daughter of former president Bill Clinton, claiming that the massacre had been 'stoked by people like you'. Owen Jones was quick to point out that the killer had recently shared an article from the *Daily Express* on social media, implying that the publication was somehow partly responsible for his actions. Although these could be well-meaning attempts to explain the inexplicable, they are no less tenuous than blaming JD Salinger for the death of John Lennon on the grounds that the murderer cited *The Catcher in the Rye* as his manifesto.

In spite of the temptation to resort to easy formulas in order to make sense of horrific acts of violence, it is neither desirable nor possible to exist in a society in which the potential to influence is regarded as a crime in and of itself. There are virtually no acts that can be undertaken in isolation from cultural factors, and any attempt to connect the dots from crime to catalyst is bound to lead us into a fog of speculation.

Surely, however, when the intention to incite violence is beyond doubt, we are right to conclude that responsibility ought to be shared. Consider the hypothetical scenario of a demagogue standing before a doting crowd. By the cheers and applause we can tell that his words have had an invigorating effect. He singles out a man on the front row and calls on the crowd to attack him. Within minutes he is dead.

While it would be folly to formulate hate speech legislation on the basis of such exceptional circumstances, it does raise the question of the degree to which authority figures should be blamed for the crimes of their followers. Charles Manson, for example, was convicted for the series of murders in 1969 committed by members of his cult. The extent to which officers at

Auschwitz should be held culpable for following orders, otherwise known as the 'Nuremberg defence', is a longstanding feature of ethical debates. On reflection, one would be hard pushed not to conclude that the responsibility lies with those who gave the orders as well as those who carried them out.

Our hypothetical scenario is slightly different, insofar as our murderers have not been following orders from an individual who has direct authority over them, but rather have been energised by his words. In this case, the distinction one must draw is between those who are inspired and those who act on that inspiration. Unlike a soldier who is commanded to carry out atrocities and punished severely if he refuses, our hypothetical lynch mob have made a free choice. Without the threat of punitive repercussions, our agency is not diminished by pressure to conform.

In the end, we have to consider which is more harmful to society: a minority who would seek to incite violence against their fellow citizens, or a state that has been empowered to set the limits of permissible thought and speech. On balance, I suspect that those of us who know a thing or two about history will settle on the latter.

The obvious counter-argument is the impact of propaganda; few would deny that the actions of Joseph Goebbels fuelled the climate of anti-Semitism in Nazi Germany, or that the 'tall trees' broadcasts in Rwanda were made in an effort to galvanise hatred. Yet again we find ourselves in the position of mitigating the personal responsibility of the assailants on the basis that they have experienced a kind of brainwashing, an assumption that human beings are readily deprived of their will by the manipulation of others. Such a proposition may or may not have merit, although it is worth noting that studies have revealed that propaganda only works if the pre-existing beliefs of the recipients are already aligned with the message.

In his overview of evidence from experimental psychology, for instance, Hugo Mercier notes that 'religious proselytizing, propaganda, advertising, and so forth are generally not very effective at changing people's minds' and that 'beliefs that lead to costly behaviour are even less likely to be accepted'. Even in the case of Nazi Germany, propaganda against Jews had the effect of exacerbating existing prejudices. In areas with low levels of anti-Semitism, propaganda had the reverse impact. This tells us that incitement to violence only occurs if the anterior circumstances have generated a climate of susceptibility. As Gordon Danning has pointed out, the academic consensus shows that hate speech does not in itself create hatred. Rather, it places 'an imprimatur of official approval on acts of violence', thereby 'making people who are already hateful and prone to violence believe that they can get away with acting violently'.

On incitement to violence, as with all complex moral issues, we should all be open to persuasion. At the same time, we must be wary of those who mistake their own arguments for proof. The connection between unfettered speech and violence is now taken by many to be self-evident, which, in turn, makes the case for hate speech irrefutable. This is to reach a conclusion intuitively and work backwards. It is exemplified by the current movement in the United States to see that hate speech is exempt from First Amendment protection.

For instance, in an article for the *New York Times* entitled 'Free Speech Is Killing Us', Andrew Marantz asserts that 'noxious language online is causing real-world violence'. He goes on to claim that 'this fact implies a question so uncomfortable that many of us go to great lengths to avoid asking it. Namely, what should we – the Government, private companies or individual citizens – be doing about it?' It should go without saying that Marantz's strategy of recasting his argument as a 'fact' does not automatically render it ironclad. The uncomfortable questions that he poses are redundant if the premise is flawed, but he has made no effort to establish whether or not this might be the case. Similarly, 'hate speech is not free speech' is a common theme on social media, but the repetition of slogans does not make them true.

This belief in a direct causal link between forms of expression and violent crime should be interrogated, not least because it is already informing various governments' justifications for hate speech legislation and politicians' pleas for the moderation of language in the media and in parliament. During a House of Commons debate in September 2019, Labour politician Paula Sheriff invoked the memory of Jo Cox – a member of parliament who had been murdered by a far-right extremist in June 2016 – in order to criticise prime minister Boris Johnson's 'pejorative language'. 'We stand here under the shield of our departed friend with many of us in this place subject to death threats and abuse every single day,' Sherriff said. 'Let me tell the prime minister they often quote his words – "surrender act", "betrayal", "traitor" – and I for one am sick of it. We must moderate our language and it has to come from the prime minister first.' In this, she was echoing Marantz's view that 'ideas can slide so precipitously into terror'. In the same debate, her colleague Jess Phillips revealed that she had received a death threat in which the prime minister's words had been quoted. But this is no proof of causality; it is merely proof that the individual who wrote the letter is capable of quotation.

The roots of this belief are probably ideological. As I have noted, present-day social justice activists share an abiding faith in the putative nexus of language and power, largely derived from the French postmodernists of the 1960s and 1970s. However, these same activists are often at the forefront of calling for the censorship of the arts, an impulse which we can trace to the thinkers of the Frankfurt School – Max Horkheimer, Theodor Adorno, Herbert Marcuse, et al. – for whom popular culture and entertainment were seen as distractions from the revolutionary project. I see in the identity-obsessed activism of today a blend of these two positions, one which reduces humanity to a passive and malleable species, eternally subject to the tides of circumstance.

Popular culture, then, becomes a means of social control, which is why 'representation' and sending the 'correct' moral message are seen as so crucial. But artists are by no means obliged to provide moral instruction, either through their lives or their work. Furthermore, to judge art by how effectively it reinforces contemporary ethical standards is entirely to misapprehend its purpose. I am reminded of Oscar Wilde's observation in his preface to *The Picture of Dorian Gray* (1890): 'There is no such thing as a moral or an immoral book. Books are well written, or badly written. That is all.'

The assumption that various forms of popular entertainment – from gory films and television to gangster rap and drill music – have the capacity to incite violence has long been a staple of tabloid sensationalism. It was the core argument of Mary Whitehouse's 'Clean Up TV' campaign in the mid-1960s. It was the rationale behind the seizure of so-called 'video nasties' in the early 1980s which, according to the England and Wales director of public prosecutions at the time, had the capacity 'to deprave and corrupt, or make morally bad, a significant propor-tion of the likely audience'. It is why Danny Boyle's film *Trainspotting* (1996) was accused of glamourising drug use. It explains the near-hysterical campaigning of the *Daily Mail* and the *Evening Standard* to have David Cronenberg's *Crash* (1996) banned in the UK, on the grounds that it was 'beyond the bounds of depravity'.

More recently, the movie *Joker* (2019) was widely decried for its potentially harmful influence on impressionable young men. One critic described it as 'a toxic rallying cry for self-pitying incels' whose director, Todd Phillips, 'lacks the discipline or nuance to responsibly handle such hazardous material'. This tone is reminiscent of the *Sunday Express* reviewer who wrote of Radclyffe Hall's book *The Well of Loneliness* (1928), 'I would rather give a healthy boy or a healthy girl a phial of prussic acid than this novel.'

For all this catastrophising, six decades of research into 'media-effects' theories has provided no secure evidence of a general correlation between public behaviour and mass-media consumption, with the 'direct-effects model' being comprehen-sively discredited. Such effects are only ever indirect and based on individual personality traits, social circumstances and moral character. This is not to suggest that there is no debate to be had regarding our susceptibility to propaganda, advertising or persuasion, or indeed that the media and the arts do not have a significant impact on culture. But the idea of a passive public acting mechanically on cues from politicians, journalists and artists appears to have little basis in reality.

In any case, I do not share the view that to restrict speech necessarily diminishes the spread of ideas. We have all heard of the 'Streisand effect', whereby attempts at censorship and suppression inadvertently draw more attention to the offending material. Whenever I hear demands for a book to be banned, my first thought is invariably: 'How can I get hold of a copy?'

The same principle applies to disinformation. The term 'fake news' is now often deployed as a strategy to delegitimise alternative viewpoints. But even in cases where deception is unambiguously the motive, censorship usually has the unintended effect of accelerating the dissemination of the material in question. Many purveyors of 'fake news' rely on the narrative that they are brave truth-tellers fighting back against oppressive forces who would see them silenced. It is therefore far better to discredit false testimony than to suppress it and thereby re-enforce disingenuous claims to victimhood.

When it comes to calls for censorship, we must always return to the same question: who are to be the censors, and how might they be expected to reach objective decisions on the basis of fundamentally subjective standards? Moreover, if speech has the power to corrupt, how can we be sure that exposure to toxic material will not corrupt the censors?

Hate Speech

———

Hatred is a human emotion that we learn to resist through the process of socialisation in youth. Our recognition of the dangers of hatred cannot eliminate the instinct and, in many cases, it may even be warranted. Is it not reasonable, even morally sound, to hate those who delight in genocide, rape and torture? Even if we are able to muster sympathy for the sociopathic, or to see them as victims of a failed system, do we not hate their acts of cruelty? Above all, are we not entitled to express this innate human impulse as and when we feel it, irrespective of whether or not the articulation of such sentiments has any moral justification?

Given these difficulties, it is clear that 'hate speech' is not something that can be meaningfully defined, a point that both the European Court of Human Rights and UNESCO have conceded. Yet as Paul Coleman outlines in his book *Censored* (2012), all European countries have hate speech laws, and 'their continued use, abuse and expansion are having a profound effect on freedom of speech across the continent'. Leaving aside the questionable morality of attempting to criminalise an emotion, how is one to set the parameters? In other words, who gets to decide what constitutes 'hate speech' in the first place?

Current guidelines by the Crown Prosecution Service define 'hate crime' as 'any criminal offence which is perceived by the victim or any other person to be motivated by hostility or prejudice, based on a person's disability or perceived disability; race or perceived race; or religion or perceived religion; or sexual orientation or perceived sexual orientation or a person who is transgender or perceived to be transgender'. Similarly, a 'hate incident' is defined as a non-criminal act that is 'perceived by the victim, or anybody else, to be motivated by hostility or prejudice based on the five protected characteristics'.

'Non-crime hate incidents' are recorded when no crime has been committed but offensive speech or behaviour has been investigated by police. This can have ramifications for the accused because these records appear on searches by the Disclosure and Barring Service (DBS), which employers are legally required to undertake. Worryingly, the *Hate Crime Operational Guidance* issued by the College of Policing instructs officers to record hateful incidents 'irrespective of whether there is any evidence to identify the hate element'.

In all of these cases, the definitions explicitly depend upon the subjective perception of the 'victim', a term that bypasses due process and presupposes guilt on the part of the accused. Where does that leave someone who has inadvertently caused offence but is perceived as having done so intentionally? As I have argued, our suspicions about other people's motives are rarely accurate, particularly at moments of heightened emotion. Besides, intuition is hardly a prudent basis for criminal prosecution.

While those who claim that we are experiencing a 'free speech crisis' may be guilty of hyperbole, they are right to draw attention to the ways in which current police procedure reveals a gradual erosion of civil liberties. Our law enforcement agencies should not be in the business of auditing our emotions. It is likewise disturbing to hear government officials – such as the Scottish justice secretary Humza Yousaf – calling for the criminalisation of speech in private dwellings. With police routinely investigating citizens for 'non-crime', and using phrases such as 'we need to check your thinking', something is most definitely awry. Although the recording of non-crime does not lead to prosecution, it nevertheless reflects this broader trend towards the politicisation of our criminal justice system and a mistrust of free speech more generally.

When the police fail to act in a politically neutral manner, they inevitably veer into authoritarianism. Three thousand people are arrested each year in the UK for offensive comments posted online, even in cases where a joke had clearly been intended. Section 127 of the Communications Act 2003 criminalises online speech that can be deemed 'grossly offensive' by the courts. Again, the requirement for a prosecutor to prove that there was any intention to cause offence is conspicuously absent.

In addition, we should be vigilant against the introduction of laws that would actually *compel* certain forms of speech. One of the most famous examples in recent years is the case of the clinical psychologist Jordan Peterson, whose refusal to be compelled to use gender-neutral pronouns led to calls for his resignation from the University of Toronto, and the possibility of legal action under Ontario's human rights code. In the UK, police investigations into 'misgendering' – the act of referring to people with gendered pronouns at odds with their identity – have been reported on numerous occasions.

In his essay 'Looking Back on the Spanish War', George Orwell imagined a 'nightmare world in which the Leader, or some ruling clique, controls not only the future but *the past*. If the Leader says of such and such an event, "It never happened" – well, it never happened. If he says that "two and two are five" – well, two and two are five. This prospect frightens me much more than bombs.' To force citizens to speak falsehoods as though they were the truth is a form of psychological control common to dictatorships. As Spinoza argued, for any man to 'be compelled to speak only according to the dictates of the supreme power' is a grievous contravention of his 'indefeasible natural right' to be 'the master of his own thoughts'.

Ultimately, the question of who gets to define 'hate speech' is insurmountable. In order to establish the parameters, one has first to navigate a set of abstract concepts – 'hate', 'offence', 'perception' – that are hopelessly subjective. Inevitably, the decision is outsourced to an authority figure or political body, one with its own biases, preferences and inherent goals of self-preservation that cannot be overcome.

Furthermore, judicial precedent is a key aspect of how the legal system operates and, if the state is willing to disregard a citizen's right to free expression, then there can be no guarantees for any of us. Even if 'hate speech' could somehow be successfully measured, the terminology will remain forever nebulous. You may trust our leaders to judge these matters sensibly, but it takes a certain myopia not to see that governments of the future might wish to abuse the precedent. Prevailing common sense offers little security against an as yet unborn state that may have perfidious, or even totalitarian, tendencies.

The price we pay for a free society is that bad people will say bad things. We tolerate this, not because we approve of the content of their speech, but because once we have compromised on the principle of free speech we clear the pathway for future tyranny.

Year Zero

Civilisation is the barricade we erect to hold back our baser instincts. This cannot be sustained without free speech and, although I do not believe we are as yet experiencing a full-blown crisis, the first fissures in the barricade are certainly widening. Media outlets and other institutions traditionally committed to liberty are wavering in the face of ideological pressure, and vocal supporters of unrestricted speech are finding themselves in the minority. Decent people with noble goals are increasingly playing a zero-sum game in which social justice is seen as only achievable if freedom of expression is deprioritised.

Even the ACLU is experiencing internal conflicts between the old guard of free speech absolutists and a new activist contingent whose ambitions seem inimical to the organisation's *raison d'être*. When even the most ardent defenders of free speech are sheering off course, it is imperative that we muster the courage to uphold this most elemental of principles. In the midst of a seemingly interminable culture war, it is always worth reiterating the point that freedom of speech is the seedbed of all our freedoms.

Many of us saw the televised images of protesters burning copies of Salman Rushdie's novel *The Satanic Verses* on the streets of Bolton and Bradford after its publication in 1988. The protests were peaceful, but there is something about the destruction of books that has a visceral and chilling effect. It isn't only that such imagery is redolent of Pathé newsreels of Joseph Goebbels addressing students in Berlin's *Opernplatz*, while brownshirts casually toss books into the flames like mere kindling. Nor is it simply the nagging sense that, had the author been present, the crowd would not have hesitated to see him suffer the same fate as his work. Above all else, the burning of books feels like a symbolic repudiation of all that our civilisation has achieved.

Rushdie felt the same, commenting that the sight of his book being 'crucified and then immolated' left him with the sense that 'now the victory of the Enlightenment was looking temporary, reversible'. If you visit the site of the Nazi bonfires in Berlin, you will find a plaque on the ground which bears a quotation from Heinrich Heine's play *Almansor* (1821). '*Dort wo man Bücher verbrennt, verbrennt man am Ende auch Menschen.*' Where they burn books, they will in the end burn people, too.

I have tried to show in this book that our best response to hateful speech is more speech. Bad ideas are not defeated when they are silenced, and making martyrs out of reprehensible people is only ever profitable to their cause. The test of our allegiance to civil liberties is our willingness to defend freedom of speech even when we find it intolerable. It is true that some who abuse their free speech will intimidate others into silence, but in censoring the abusive individual we lose the opportunity to expose the iniquity of their beliefs through public admonition.

Worse still, we risk setting a precedent that the powerful and the moralistic will be only too willing to exploit. For the sake of short-term gains, we end up sabotaging a principle that protects us all.

Debate is not, as some have asserted, a 'fetish'. It is the means by which we forestall the closing of our minds. We argue to refine our point of view, to challenge our certainties, and to persuade others when we feel that they are misguided. In order to do this, we must be able to understand our opponent's perspective, and not satisfy ourselves with crude misrepresentations. Above all, we argue because we know, even when we are not willing to admit, that there is always the possibility that we might be wrong. We are not infallible, and we can be sure that much of the received wisdom of the present will be derided by our descendants.

The conservation of freedom of speech, then, is as much an exercise in self-interest as a commitment to universal liberty. In this, we might look to the words of Thomas Paine: 'I have always strenuously supported the Right of every Man to his own opinion, however different that opinion might be to mine. He who denies to another this right, makes a slave of himself to his present opinion, because he precludes himself the right of changing it'.

The same utopian instinct that would see 'problematic' ideas purged in the present has resulted in numerous attempts to sanitise the past. In 2020, the British Library's 'Decolonising Working Group' advised the institution to 'powerfully reinterpret' statues of the founders, replace maps that are 'Eurocentric' and review material in its collections that promotes the 'outdated notion' of Western civilisation. They even went so far as to claim that the architecture of the library building is offensively imperialist because it resembles a battleship.

Across the country, many university and school curricula are being 'decolonised' of authors and works on the basis of identity politics or moral purity. There have been calls to demolish statues of historical figures with ties to the slave trade, such as Edward Coulston or Cecil Rhodes. But there have been more surprising targets, such as monuments to Mahatma Gandhi and Abraham Lincoln. Cancel culture is not limited to the living.

Debates surrounding these issues are complicated, and perspectives vary depending on whether these monuments are deemed to be celebratory in nature or remnants of a history that we would be unwise to forget. But wherever one stands on the issue, it is important to note that the totalitarian mindset has always been revisionist in nature, so we are right to be cautious about where such actions might eventually lead.

The Internet is a revolution of the written word to rival the invention of the printing press, enabling our ideas to reach a far wider audience than ever before. But as this new means of expression has proliferated, we face unprecedented threats that would see our liberties rescinded. A combination of state censorship, hostility to press freedom, cancel culture, big tech interference, media complacency, and a substantial proportion of the public that has lost trust in its fellow citizens, has created the conditions within which authoritarian alternatives can germinate. That much of this is well intentioned does not mitigate the threat, it only makes it more difficult to combat without being mischaracterised as a reactionary.

It is remarkable that 'hate speech', a concept that is frankly impossible to define, should be taken as axiomatic. Those who assert that hatred should be beyond the purview of free speech protections are usually carving out exceptions for ideas that they find troubling or distasteful. If their concern is harassment, threats, defamation and other forms of speech-related crimes, they should be consoled by the fact that these are already illegal and require no additional legislation. That so many states persist in passing new laws on the basis of 'hate' is a grave cause for concern as there can be no guarantee that such amorphous and subjective terminology will not lead to the criminalisation of unpopular opinions or legitimate criticism of those in power. On balance, it is clear that the entire notion of 'hate speech' has no place in the statute books of a liberal democracy.

Most people agree that state censorship is rarely a force for good. Of course, there will always be those whose instinct inclines towards submission to authority, who are happy to shift beliefs in accordance with the fashion or decrees from above. Orwell called this the 'gramophone mind', content to play the record of the moment whether or not one is in agreement. It is an enervated and dehumanised public that acquiesces to the paternalism of their leaders. By contrast, to resist state censorship is to take a wrecking ball to the panopticon. As Eduard Bernstein so succinctly put it, 'men have heads', and we only enfeeble ourselves if we neglect to use them.

The capacity to articulate our thoughts is how we engage with the world; it is the essence of our common humanity. To grapple with the complexities of life is a collaborative endeavour. Without freedom of speech, therefore, we are kept in a permanent state of infancy, thwarted in our development as fully autonomous and free-thinking citizens. Without it, there can be no education, no means to defend ourselves when maligned or misrepresented, no exchange of ideas, no artistic expression, and no safeguard against indoctrination. Through speech we express scepticism, probe for answers, make sense of our experiences, and navigate towards the ever-receding horizon of truth. We surrender these freedoms at our peril.

The warnings of history are there should we wish to heed them. Our liberties have been hard won, and those who attack them now are only able to do because of the privileges they afford. There is no edifice sufficiently robust that it will not eventually yield to sustained pressure. We are right to distrust those who assume their own infallibility and moral superiority over the past, who consider their small pocket of existence to be a kind of Year Zero in the grand narrative of humanity.

Thirty years ago, any would-be Cassandra would have been derided had she claimed that a time would come when police would routinely investigate citizens for 'non-crime', when students would be demanding protection from unpleasant ideas, or when mainstream politicians would be calling for the criminalisation of private conversations in the home. Such prognostications would simply have been dismissed outright. Yet here we are.

It may be that in another thirty years we will have resigned ourselves to self-censorship and conformity to the status quo. Perhaps all art will be a form of ideological reinforcement, with eccentricity and free-thinking seen as quirks of a half-forgotten time. Perhaps we will learn to live under the continual supervision of the state, tempering our every utterance in accordance with the accepted script. Such a scenario seems inconceivable to those who have not learned the lessons of the past. For the rest of us, it is surely worth stemming the momentum of this new illiberalism. While we should celebrate progress, we need to be able to recognise the forces of regression that usurp its name. Even if we fail, at least we can say we tried.

Acknowledgements

My thanks to Andreas Campomar and his colleagues at Constable for helping to bring this book to life. I would also like to thank David Butterfield and Martin Gourlay for their invaluable feedback on early drafts and for spotting most of my errors.

I am grateful to all those organisations upholding freedom of speech at a time when there are so many who would see our liberties curbed. In the UK, these include the Academy of Ideas, Index on Censorship and the Free Speech Union. I owe a special debt of gratitude to the team at *spiked* magazine, who have published most of my writing on free speech over the past few years.

Thanks also to Paul Baker, Matthew Hamilton and Philip Doherty.

Notes

'We Need to Check Your Thinking'

p.1   **'We need to check your thinking':** Camilla Tominey and Joani Walsh, 'Man investigated by police for retweeting transgender limerick', the *Telegraph* (24 January 2019). Miller eventually decided to bring a court case against the College of Policing, whose Hate Crime Operational Guidance (HCOG), issued in 2014, forms the basis of current practice. As he argued at the High Court, 'The idea that a law-abiding citizen can have their name recorded against a hate incident on a crime report when there was neither hate nor crime undermines principles of justice, free expression, democracy and common sense.' Ultimately, the police response was judged to be unlawful, although the High Court rejected Miller's challenge against the lawfulness of the College of Policing guidelines. See Izzy Lyons, '"Right to be offended" does not exist, judge says as court hears police record hate incidents even if there is no evidence,' the *Telegraph* (20 November 2019).

p.2   **'non-crime hate incidents':** Izzy Lyons, Jack Hardy and Martin Evans, 'Police record 120,000 "non-crime" hate incidents that may stop accused getting jobs', the *Telegraph* (15 February 2020).

p.3   **'the name Franz Kafka':** Christopher Hitchens, *Hitch-22: A Memoir* (London: Atlantic Books, 2010), p. 337.

p.3   **'had no need to know the reason':** Ibid., p. 338.

p.3   **'they make you do it':** Christopher Hitchens, 'The Axis of Evil', lecture delivered at the Center for American Studies at the University of Western Ontario (9 April 2005).

FREE SPEECH

p.3 **'struggle between Liberty and Authority':** John Stuart Mill, *On Liberty* (London: Everyman's Library, 1992), p. 5. Originally published in 1859.

p.4 **printed texts passed before a censor:** John Milton, *Areopagitica: A speech for the liberty of unlicensed printing, to the parliament of England* (1644), in *The Complete English Poems* (London: Everyman's Library, 1992), ed. Gordon Campbell, pp. 573–618. Quotation taken from p. 602. This edition also includes the text of the Licensing Order of 14 June 1643 (pp. 619–620). The title is a reference to the *Areopagiticus*, a speech by the Greek orator Isocrates (436–338 BC), although this has caused some confusion given that Isocrates wanted to reinstate the court of the Areopagus as the censor of public indecency and immorality, which seems incongruous in relation to Milton's stated objectives.

p.4 **'thinking in astronomy':** Ibid., p. 602.

Left and Right

p.6 **'a term the far right wilfully abuse':** Owen Jones, '"Tommy Robinson" is no martyr to freedom of speech', the *Guardian* (31 May 2018).

p.6 **'no reasoning without speech':** Thomas Hobbes, *Leviathan*, ed. AP Martinich (Peterborough, Canada: Broadway Press, 2002), p. 30. Originally published in 1651.

Then and Now

p.9 **'speaking truth with candour':** The earliest recorded usage of the term *parrhesia* is by the tragedian Euripides in the *Hippolytus* of 428 BC.

p.10 **a resurgence in Europe:** For a compelling account of this development, I would recommend Charles G Nauert, Jr, *Humanism and the Culture of Renaissance Europe* (Cambridge: Cambridge University Press, 1995).

p.10 **regulations on the press:** Even today many regimes – e.g. Thailand, Cambodia, Morocco and Saudi Arabia – retain *lèse majesté* laws in order to punish criticism of the king. In recent years, President Recep Tayyip Erdoğan of Turkey reinstated obscure laws that have resulted in the prosecution of thousands of people who have offended him. These include Merve Büyüksaraç, a former beauty queen who, in 2016, was convicted for posting a satirical poem about Erdoğan on Instagram. In the same year, the Turkish authorities called for the prosecution of the German comedian Jan Böhmermann for producing a video that characterised Erdoğan as a sexual deviant.

p.11 **'freedom of the press':** Quoted by Richard J Evans, *The Coming of the Third Reich* (London: Allen Lane, 2003), p. 333.

p.11 *ransacking houses for books to burn*: George Orwell, *Nineteen Eighty-Four* (London: Secker & Warburg, 1949); Ray Bradbury, *Fahrenheit 451* (New York: Ballantine Books, 1953).

p.11 *illegal conduct by journalists:* Not a single national newspaper agreed to sign up to the press regulating body IMPRESS (Independent Monitor for the Press) which had been established in the wake of the Leveson Inquiry (2011–12) commissioned by the UK Government. Irrespective of their political leanings, the publications were united in their opposition to Section 40 of the Crime and Courts Act, which was intended to curb the abusive excesses of the industry. In particular, they were concerned because the legislation would see them liable to pay all legal costs in litigation cases even if they won. This would make investigative journalism especially hazardous as any resultant lawsuits could be financially crippling, a situation likely to be exploited by those who wish to silence critical voices.

p.11 *free speech battles of the digital age:* Free speech protections outside of constitutional law are more explicitly afforded by Article 19 of the United Nations' Universal Declaration of Human Rights: 'Everyone has the right to freedom of opinion and expression; this right includes freedom to hold opinions without interference and to seek, receive and impart information and ideas through any media and regardless of frontiers.'

p.12 *'Twitter stands for freedom of expression'*: Jack Dorsey, Twitter (5 October 2015).

p.12 *this commendable ideal no longer applies:* Josh Halliday, 'Twitter's Tony Wang: "We are the free-speech wing of the free-speech party"', the *Guardian* (22 March 2012); David Streitfeld, '"The Internet is broken": @ev is trying to salvage it', the *New York Times* (20 May 2017).

p.13 *partisan censorship:* Douglas Murray has noted how this bias is reflected even in the selection criteria for employees for these social media companies. Applicants are tested in order 'to weed out anyone with the wrong ideological inclinations'. The major tech giants, Murray writes, employ 'thousands of people on six-figure salaries whose job it is to try to formulate and police content'. Douglas Murray, *The Madness of Crowds* (London: Bloomsbury, 2019), pp. 110–111.

Common Misapprehensions

p.16 *'the fallacy of demanding to be heard':* Helen Pluckrose and James Lindsay, 'Freedom of speech and the fallacy of demanding to be heard', *New Discourses* (22 January 2020).

p.16   *a pernicious underlying intention is . . . assumed:* The metaphor of the 'dog whistle' is an accusation that someone is disguising their objectionable views by sending signals that only the likeminded will register, much as human beings remain oblivious to the higher sound frequencies that dogs are able to hear.

p.16   *'racist ideas and racialising claims':* Gavan Titley, *Is Free Speech Racist?* (Cambridge: Polity Press, 2020), p. 12.

p.17   *protect the rights of the most vulnerable in society:* This is the main thesis of Suzanne Nossel's book *Dare to Speak*, in which she reminds us that 'the quest for a diverse, inclusive society is in fact fortified by the defense of free speech, and the case for free speech is more credible and more persuasive when it incorporates a defense of equality as well'. Suzanne Nossel, *Dare to Speak: Defending Free Speech for All* (New York: Dey Street, 2020), p. 4.

p.17   *in countries where free speech protections are meagre:* Jacob Mchangama, 'We need to defend the right to offend', *National Review* (14 February 2015).

p.17   *the likes of Daryl Davis:* Sam Harris relates an anecdote which also shows the redemptive power of talking to the intolerable. 'I remember hearing about a rabbi who was receiving threatening calls from a white supremacist. Rather than hang up or call the police, the rabbi patiently heard the man out, every time he called, whatever the hour. Eventually they started having a real conversation, and ultimately the rabbi broke through, and the white supremacist started telling him about all the troubles in his life. They even met and become friends. One certainly likes to believe that such breakthroughs are possible.' Sam Harris, *Lying* (Los Angeles: Four Elephants Press, 2013), p. 46.

p.18   *'he establishes a precedent that will reach to himself':* Thomas Paine, 'Dissertation on First-Principles of Government', in *The Writings of Thomas Paine*, 4 vols. (New York: GP Putnam's Sons, 1894–96), ed. Moncure Daniel Conway, 3, pp. 256–277. Quotation taken from p. 277. This anticipates Orwell's comment that 'if you encourage totalitarian methods, the time may come when they will be used against you instead of for you'. George Orwell, 'The freedom of the press', in *Essays* (London: Everyman's Library, 2002), ed. Peter Davison, pp. 888–897. Quotation taken from pp. 894–895.

p.19   *'the only way to protect a free society':* Aryeh Neier, *Defending My Enemy: American Nazis, the Skokie Case, and the Risks of Freedom* (New York: Dutton, 1979), pp. 1–2.

The Social Contract

p.21   *'claims about the inviolability of free expression are humbug':* Yasmin Alibhai-Brown and Simon Heffer, 'Is "political correctness" a force for good?', *Prospect* (18 October 2018).

p.22 *the essentially co-operative nature of human society:* Jean-Jacques Rousseau's *The Social Contract* was first published as *Du contrat social; ou Principes du droit politique* in 1762.

p.23 *'falsely shouting "Fire!" in a theatre':* Quoted by Kenan Malik, 'Shadow of the fatwa', *Index on Censorship*, vol. 37, no. 4 (November 2008), pp. 112–120.

p.23 *the 'crowded theatre' argument is 'worse than useless':* Gabe Rottman, 'A "foreign policy exception" to the First Amendment?', *ACLU* (28 September 2012).

Cancel Culture

p.25 *'cancel culture' . . . typically driven by social media:* In his book, *So You've Been Publicly Shamed*, Jon Ronson traces the re-emergence of public shaming as a form of justice brought about by the rise of social media. This was written before the term 'cancel culture' became prevalent. Jon Ronson, *So You've Been Publicly Shamed* (London: Picador, 2015).

p.25 *'gaslighting':* This concept of 'gaslighting' takes its name from the 1940 movie *Gaslight*, in which a husband convinces his wife that she is going insane by, among other things, dimming the lights and then denying that the house is getting darker when she complains.

p.26 *open letter in* **Harper's Magazine:** 'A letter on justice and open debate', *Harper's Magazine* (7 July 2020).

p.26 *gender self-identification might compromise women-only spaces:* Rowling's concerns stem from her own experience as a survivor of domestic abuse, a position she outlined in a blog posted on her website on 10 June 2020.

p.26 *some have nonetheless interpreted her views as hostile:* In a series of tweets posted on 7 June 2020, Rowling explained her position: 'If sex isn't real, there's no same-sex attraction. If sex isn't real, the lived reality of women globally is erased. I know and love trans people, but erasing the concept of sex removes the ability of many to meaningfully discuss their lives. It isn't hate to speak the truth. The idea that women like me, who've been empathetic to trans people for decades, feeling kinship because they're vulnerable in the same way as women – i.e., to male violence – "hate" trans people because they think sex is real and has lived consequences – is a nonsense. I respect every trans person's right to live any way that feels authentic and comfortable to them. I'd march with you if you were discriminated against on the basis of being trans. At the same time, my life has been shaped by being female. I do not believe it's hateful to say so.'

p.26 **a biological basis to womanhood:** Much of the furore began after Rowling supported tax expert Maya Forstater, who had been dismissed by her employers for disagreeing with the Government's proposed amendments to the Gender Recognition Act. After Forstater lost her tribunal, Rowling tweeted the hashtag #IStandWithMaya and said: 'Dress however you please. Call yourself whatever you like. Sleep with any consenting adult who'll have you. Live your best life in peace and security. But force women out of their jobs for stating that sex is real?'

p.26 **a vocal minority have bombarded her with abuse:** Many of the most abusive public online messages that Rowling received were collated on the website *Medium* on 9 June 2020 under the title 'JK Rowling and the trans activists: a story in screenshots'.

p.27 **'mercy's antithesis':** Nick Cave, 'Why cancel culture destroys the creative soul', *Spectator* (31 December 2020).

p.27 **'JK Rowling isn't being cancelled':** Emma Kelly, 'JK Rowling isn't being cancelled, she's just facing the consequences of her actions', *Metro* (10 July 2020).

p.27 **Gillian Philip was dropped by her publisher:** Jack Haugh, 'Scots author Gillian Philip dumped for backing JK Rowling in transgender row', the *Herald* (6 July 2020).

p.27 **'people seem to think freedom of speech means "saying things without being challenged"':** Owen Jones, Twitter (8 July 2020).

p.27 **'freedom of speech means freedom from objection':** Nesrine Malik, 'The myth of the free speech crisis', the *Guardian* (3 September 2019).

p.28 **free speech 'doesn't mean the right to say what you want without rebuttal':** Reni Eddo-Lodge, *Why I'm No Longer Talking to White People About Race* (London: Bloomsbury Circus, 2017), p. 134.

p.28 **stories about people who have been hounded out of work:** Examples of cancel culture could fill a whole other volume, but the following are a selection that have been widely reported in the media.

   In June 2015, the Nobel Prize-winning biochemist Tim Hunt was forced to resign from his honorary position at University College London after a journalist misrepresented jokes he had made at a conference in Seoul, South Korea.

   In April 2019, philosopher Roger Scruton was sacked as housing adviser to the Conservative Government (as part of the Building Better, Building Beautiful Commission) after a journalist at the *New Statesman* doctored his statements in an interview in order to make them appear racist.

   In June 2019, ASDA supermarket worker Brian Leach was fired after sharing a video online by the comedian Billy Connolly that mocked Islamic suicide bombers, even though the source of the offending excerpt was from a DVD sold by the company that employed him. He was later reinstated following an outcry.

In August 2019, schoolteacher Christian Webb lost his job when it emerged that he had performed in viral comedy rap videos under the pseudonym 'MC Devvo' in the mid-2000s.

In January 2020, veteran television presenter Alastair Stewart was forced to resign after tweeting a quotation from Shakespeare which included the phrase 'an angry ape'. This was misinterpreted as racist because he was replying to a black Twitter user, even though it was a phrase he had used previously in conversation with white people.

In June 2020, Nick Buckley, the founder of charity organisation Mancunian Way, which is committed to helping young people from ethnic minority backgrounds to find work, was ousted for criticising the radical politics of the Black Lives Matter movement (most notably their calls to defund the police and abolish capitalism). Although Buckley's opposition to racism was never in doubt, the charity capitulated to pressure from online campaigners who smeared him as racist and demanded his dismissal. It was only after a petition and counter-campaign that the decision was reversed.

In August 2020, Sasha White, an assistant at the Tobias Literary Agency in New York, was fired after a campaign by trans activists who took offence at statements posted on her private Twitter account expressing her view that gender-neutral pronouns were unhelpful to the feminist cause.

p.28 **they believe their employment prospects would be endangered:** *Cato Institute Summer 2020 National Survey* (July 2020).

p.30 **her voice was erased from the game:** Helen Lewis, 'A man can't just say he has turned into a woman', the *Times* (25 July 2020).

p.30 **'[we] will reinforce our background checks for partners in the future':** *Watch Dogs Legion: News*, Twitter (7 November 2020).

The Indispensable Condition

p.31 **government-enforced restrictions on speech:** A poll for the Pew Research Center in 2015 found that 40 per cent of people between the ages of 18 and 34 were in favour of the government prohibiting speech that is offensive towards minority groups. The statistics declined according to age range; the figure for those aged between 35 and 50 was 27 per cent, between 51 and 69 it was 24 per cent, and between 70 and 87 it was 12 per cent. See Richard Wike and Katie Simmons, *Global Support for Principle of Free Expression, but Opposition to Some Forms of Speech*, Pew Research Center (November 2015). A study by the Policy Exchange think-tank in 2019 revealed that fewer than half of university students in the UK consistently support freedom of speech. According to the findings, 41 per cent agreed with Cambridge University's decision to rescind the fellowship of Canadian psychologist Jordan Peterson, as opposed to 31 per cent who disagreed. The invitation had prompted a backlash from the student body, and eventually the decision was reversed. According to a university spokeswoman, this had originally been justified on the grounds that Peterson's opinions would be a threat to their 'inclusive environment'. The study also found that many UK students disapproved of Cardiff University's decision to overrule the activists who sought to have Germaine Greer disinvited in 2015 for her supposedly transphobic views; 44 per cent opposed the university's intervention, whereas 35 per cent supported it.

p.32 *the far right is experiencing a resurgence:* Statistics quoted in a report by the United States Government Accountability Office, *Countering Violent Extremism: Actions Needed to Define Strategy and Assess Progress of Federal Efforts* (April 2017), confirm that attacks motivated by far-right extremism are on the rise. For further analysis of this data see Jack Buckby, *Monster of their Own Making: How the Far Left, the Media, and Politicians are Creating Far-Right Extremists* (New York: Bombardier Books, 2020), pp. 62–66. See also Rakib Ehsan and Paul Stott (eds.), *Countering the Far Right: An Anthology* (London: Henry Jackson Society, 2020).

p.33 *a tendency to discard, or entirely misrepresent, statistics:* A recent investigation into racism at UK universities by the *Guardian* gives us an example of how research can be interpreted to prove the opposite of what it reveals. Data collected from 131 universities demonstrated that from 2014 to 2019 there were 996 formal complaints of racism, of which 367 were upheld. This means that, on average, there were only 1.5 formal complaints of racism each year in any given institution, with only 73 upheld complaints among a university population that runs into the millions. The *Guardian*'s headline told a different story: 'Revealed: the scale of racism at universities'. According to the article, the data constitutes 'widespread evidence of discrimination' and shows that racism in higher education is 'endemic'. A follow-up comment piece declared that the study 'demonstrates a lack of progress that borders on the obstinate'. In other words, a study whose findings conclusively prove that racism in universities is vanishingly rare was being taken as evidence of endemic racism. See David Batty, 'UK universities condemned for failure to tackle racism', the *Guardian* (5 July 2019) and Lola Okolosie, 'No wonder UK universities are failing on racism – most don't value diversity at all', the *Guardian* (8 July 2019).

p.33 *the memorable words of Benjamin Cardozo:* Quoted by Nossel, op. cit., p. 258.

p.33   *the Free Speech Movement:* For instance, in his introduction to *Unsafe Space*, a collection of essays on campus censorship, Tom Slater contrasts the 'spirit of '64' with the 'new intolerance' of present-day university speech codes. Tom Slater (ed.), *Unsafe Space: The Crisis of Free Speech on Campus* (London: Palgrave Macmillan, 2016), pp. 1–4.

p.33   *'the very dignity of what a human being is':* Quoted by Greg Lukianoff and Jonathan Haidt, *The Coddling of the American Mind: How Good Intentions and Bad Ideas Are Setting Up a Generation for Failure* (London: Allen Lane, 2018), p. 84.

Offence

p.37   *nobody . . . knowingly desires evil things:* See Peter Boghossian and James Lindsay, *How to Have Impossible Conversations: A Very Practical Guide* (New York: Lifelong Books, 2019), pp. 24–28. The authors draw on Plato's *Meno* to address the problem of the natural human inclination to assume the worst motives in those who do not share our views. 'If you must make an assumption about your partner's intentions,' they write, 'make only one: their intentions are better than you think.' (p. 28). John Stuart Mill describes this as the tendency 'to stigmatise those who hold the contrary opinion as bad and immoral men'. Mill, op. cit., p. 53.

p.37   *'emotional and intellectual comfort as though it were a right':* Greg Lukianoff, *Freedom from Speech* (New York: Encounter Books, 2014), pp. 12–13.

A Thought Experiment

p.42   *a substantial minority remain unpersuaded of the validity of gay marriage:* A poll by the Pew Research Center in 2019 found that 31 per cent of American adults oppose gay marriage.

p.42   *a debate about whether or not slavery is morally acceptable:* Speaking in the House of Commons on 5 February 2013, Labour MP Stephen Doughty acknowledged that the comparison of the gay marriage question with slavery was potentially 'crude' and 'crass' but nevertheless identified what he perceived to be 'important historical parallels in the development of Christian and non-Christian views on these issues'. As he put it, 'Slavery and same-sex marriage are different issues, but I hope the House today moves on in its conception, towards people of all sexualities. I also hope we move towards the state – and, I hope in time, more faiths – being able to open up the offer of the commitment signified by marriage' (Hansard).

p.42   *the issue of gay rights:* Homosexuality was decriminalised in England and Wales in 1967 and in Scotland in 1980. The age of consent was equalised in 2001. Section 28 (the law prohibiting the 'promotion' of homosexuality in schools) was repealed in 2003. Gay marriage was legalised in the UK in 2014 and in Northern Ireland in 2020.

p.42 *the cultural specificity of ethical norms:* The 'Overton Window' is named after Joseph P Overton, who first conceived the idea in relation to the opinions expressed by politicians and how they would be received.

p.43 *'people stick to an opinion that they have long supported':* William Hazlitt, 'Belief, whether voluntary?' in *Literary Remains*, 2 vols. (London: Saunders and Otley, 1836), I, pp. 83–96. Quotation taken from p. 86. This was a posthumous publication, as Hazlitt died in 1830.

p.43 *'a soul of truth in things erroneous':* Herbert Spencer, *First Principles*, sixth edition (London: Watts & Co, 1937), p. 3. First edition published in 1862.

p.44 *'the unimpeachably good' and 'the irredeemably bad':* Rabbi Jonathan Sacks, *Not in God's Name: Confronting Religious Violence* (New York: Random House, 2015), p. 51.

p.44 *the metaphor of sunlight being the best disinfectant:* 'Wrong opinions and practices gradually yield to fact and argument; but facts and arguments, to produce any effect on the mind, must be brought before it.' Mill, op. cit., p. 22.

p.44 *'let her and Falsehood grapple':* Milton, op. cit., p. 613.

p.44 *the best way to achieve this is to listen and to read:* 'Since therefore the knowledge and survey of vice is in this world so necessary to the constituting of human virtue, and the scanning of error to the confirmation of truth, how can we more safely, and with less danger, scout into the regions of sin and falsity than by reading all manner of tractates, and hearing all manner of reason? And this is the benefit which may be had of books promiscuously read.' Ibid., p. 590.

p.45 *'a dead dogma, not a living truth':* Mill, op. cit., p. 35.

p.45 *it has a glamourising effect that, if anything, enhances their appeal:* As Francis Bacon put it: 'The punishing of wits enhances their authority, and a forbidden writing is thought to be a certain spark of truth that flies up in the faces of them who seek to tread it out.' Quoted by Milton, op. cit., p. 604.

p.46 *'potential to generate other targets for censorship':* Brendan O'Neill, 'From No Platform to Safe Space: A Crisis of Enlightenment', in Slater, op. cit., pp. 5–21. Quotation taken from p. 9.

p.47 *'the right to tell people what they do not want to hear':* Orwell, 'The freedom of the press', in Davison, op. cit., pp. 888–897. Quotation taken from p. 897.

Comedy and Satire

p.50   *satirists are particularly likely to transgress the limits of acceptable discourse:* To my mind, the most succinct summary of the distinction between comedy and satire is that of WH Auden in his introduction to Byron's *Selected Poetry and Prose* (London: New English Library, 1966). 'Satire is angry and optimistic – it believes that the evil it attacks can be abolished; comedy is good-tempered and pessimistic – it believes that however much we may wish we could, we cannot change human nature and must make the best of a bad job.'

p.50   *'I would rather die standing than live on my knees':* 'A Charlie Hebdo, on n'a "pas l'impression d'égorger quelqu'un avec un feutre"', Le Monde (20 September 2012).

p.50   *'insensitive toward the Muslim faith':* Angela Charlton, 'AP explains: why does France incite anger in the Muslim world?', *Associated Press* (31 October 2020). The title of the article was later changed to 'AP explains: why France sparks such anger in Muslim world'.

p.50   *'France's dangerous religion of secularism':* Farhad Khosrokhavar, 'France's dangerous religion of secularism', *Politico* (31 October 2020). The article was eventually taken down from the *Politico* website following a backlash, and a statement was issued to the effect that the article did not meet their editorial standards. Perhaps most incendiary of all was a sentence which appeared to hold the victims responsible for their fate: 'They should have thought more carefully about their words.'

p.51   *'we owe it to ourselves to act with respect for others':* Kim Willsher, 'Nice police question man over reported contact with basilica suspect', the *Guardian* (30 October 2020).

p.51   *a lingering sense that the victims were to blame:* On 29 October 2020, the former prime minister of Malaysia, Mahathir Mohamad, tweeted that 'Muslims have a right to be angry and to kill millions of French people for the massacres of the past.' Pakistan's prime minister Imran Khan blamed the radicalisation of Islamic terrorists on the French president Emmanuel Macron's tolerance for the right of citizens to blaspheme against Islam. On 25 October 2020, Khan tweeted: 'President Macron has chosen to deliberately provoke Muslims, incl his own citizens, through encouraging the display of blasphemous cartoons targeting Islam & our Prophet PBUH. By attacking Islam, clearly without having any understanding of it, President Macron has attacked & hurt the sentiments of millions of Muslims in Europe & across the world. The last thing the world wants or needs is further polarisation. Public statements based on ignorance will create more hate, Islamophobia & space for extremists.' The president of Turkey, Recep Tayyip Erdoğan, claimed that 'Macron needs some sort of mental treatment. What else is there to say about a head of state who doesn't believe in the freedom of religion and behaves this way against the millions of people of different faiths living in his own country?' See Gul Tuysuz, Martin Goillandeau and Zamira Rahim, 'France condemns "unacceptable" comments from Turkey's Erdogan and recalls ambassador', *CNN* (26 October 2020).

p.51 **the natural and ineluctable human tendency to take offence:** Any serious attempt to legislate against the causing of offence would have to reckon with the offence caused by those who would lose their freedom to speak under such a system. If subjective notions of what is 'offensive' are to be the benchmark, then the goal to limit offence by legislation is literally impossible.

p.51 **'God is only sacred to those who believe in him':** Stéphane Charbonnier, *Open Letter: On Blasphemy, Islamophobia, and the True Enemies of Free Expression* (London: Little, Brown, 2016), pp. 15–16. Originally published as *Lettres aux escrocs de l'islamophobie qui font le jeu des racistes* (Paris: Les Échappés, 2015).

p.51 **the false impression that the magazine routinely 'punches down' at minority ethnic groups:** After the massacre, PEN America (an organisation committed to the celebration and defence of writers' free speech) awarded *Charlie Hebdo* a freedom of expression award. More victim-blaming ensued when thirty-five writers signed a letter protesting against the decision on the grounds that the magazine had mocked a 'section of the French population that is already marginalized, embattled and victimized'. See Alan Yuhas, 'Two dozen writers join Charlie Hebdo PEN award protest', the *Guardian* (29 April 2015).

p.51 **Charlie Hebdo's critics have a number of shared qualities:** Robert McLiam Wilson, 'The scurrilous lies written about Charlie Hebdo', the *Guardian* (3 January 2016).

p.53 **'sticking a clown nose on Marx':** Charbonnier, op. cit., p. 17.

p.53 **to excoriate these cartoonists for racism:** Writing in the *Guardian*, Jonathan Freedland offered a similarly uncharitable interpretation of a cartoon in *Charlie Hebdo* of the drowned refugee child Aylan Kurdi which, he felt, implied that he 'would have grown up to be a sexual abuser like those immigrants allegedly involved in the assaults in Cologne'. Yet in the same article he acknowledges the true target of the satire, which is 'the fickleness of the great European public and press, overflowing with tears for a child in August, baring its teeth in anger at the criminals of Cologne in January'. Freedland even went so far as to claim that the cartoon 'isn't satirical', a self-evidently unsustainable proposition. See Jonathan Freedland, 'Charlie Hebdo's refugee cartoon isn't satirical. It's inflammatory', the *Guardian* (15 January 2016).

NOTES

The Self-Censoring Artist

p.56 **the views of the creative industries' many gatekeepers:** Many publishers now employ 'sensitivity readers' to vet authors' work with the aim of identifying and excising any material that might be deemed offensive. Once limited to children's books, sensitivity readers are now being enlisted to monitor fiction intended for adult consumption.

p.56 **'life seen through a temperament':** Zola's phrase is '*un coin de la création vu à travers un tempérament*'. See Émile Zola, *Mes Haines: Causeries Littéraires et Artistiques* (Paris: Achille Faure, 1866), p. 25. It is paraphrased as 'life seen through a temperament' by Forrest Reid in his novel *Brian Westby* (London: Faber & Faber, 1934), pp. 165–166.

p.57 **once artists begin tailoring their work:** In *Two Cheers for Democracy*, EM Forster offered a cogent defence of the artist and his right to free expression. 'He is not like the mystic; he cannot function in a vacuum, he cannot spin tales in his head or paint pictures in the air, or hum tunes under his breath. He must have an audience, he must express his feelings, and if he knows he may be forbidden to express himself, he becomes afraid to feel. Officials, even when they are well-meaning, do not realise this. Their make-up is so different. They assume that when a book is censored only the book in question is affected. They do not realise that they may have impaired the creative machinery of the writer's mind, and prevented him from writing good books in the future.' EM Forster, *Two Cheers For Democracy* (London: Edward Arnold, 1951), pp. 44.

p.57 **'he may regard it as a commercial experiment':** Forrest Reid, *Crying for Elysium: Stories, Poems, Essays* (Richmond: Valancourt Books, 2017), ed. Andrew Doyle, p. 403.

p.57 **adherence to what Mill described as the 'despotism of custom':** Mill, op. cit., p. 68.

p.58 **individuality can only flourish in times of leisure:** Oscar Wilde, 'The Soul of Man Under Socialism', in *Plays, Prose Writings and Poems* (London: Everyman's Library, 1991), pp. 389–421.

p.58 **'the embryo music dead in his throat':** RS Thomas, 'The Welsh Hill Country', in *Collected Poems: 1945–1990* (London: Phoenix, 2000), p. 22.

The New Conformity

p.59 **extremely few 'are afraid to utter their political opinions in public':** George Orwell, 'The English people', in Davison, op. cit., pp. 608–648. Quotation taken from p. 620.

p.59 *one's true opinions are withheld:* Timur Kuran, *Private Truths, Public Lies: The Social Consequences of Preference Falsification* (Cambridge, Massachusetts: Harvard University Press, 1995).

p.60 *'if you set your face against custom':* William Hazlitt, 'On thought and action', in *Table Talk* (London: Everyman's Library, 1959), pp. 101–113. Quotation taken from p. 103. Originally published in 1821.

p.60 *an artificial reality:* Even once lies are exposed, it is common for us to find it difficult to remember anything other than the original falsehood. Psychologists call this the 'illusory truth effect'.

p.60 *and thereby beget a flock of industrious sheep:* I have borrowed this image from Alexis de Tocqueville. 'After having thus taken each individual one by one into its powerful hands, and having molded him as it pleases, the sovereign power extends its arms over the entire society; it covers the surface of society with a network of small, complicated, minute, and uniform rules, which the most original minds and the most vigorous souls cannot break through to go beyond the crowd; it does not break wills, but it softens them, bends them and directs them; it rarely forces action, but it constantly opposes your acting; it does not destroy, it prevents birth; it does not tyrannize, it hinders, it represses, it enervates, it extinguishes, it stupefies, and finally it reduces each nation to being nothing more than a flock of timid and industrious animals, of which the government is the shepherd.' See Alexis de Tocqueville, *Democracy in America*, 4 vols. (London: Saunders & Otley, 1835–40).

p.60 *'the tyranny of the prevailing opinion and feeling':* Mill, op. cit., p. 8.

p.60 *a cogent vindication of the primacy of the individual:* 'Over himself, over his own body and mind, the individual is sovereign.' Ibid., p. 13.

p.61 *less than 12 per cent of academic staff are right-leaning:* Noah Carl, *Lackademia: Why Do Academics Lean Left?* (London: Adam Smith Institute, 2017).

p.61 *one in three conservative scholars claim to self-censor:* *Academic Freedom in the UK: Protecting Viewpoint Diversity* (London: Policy Exchange, 2020). A recent survey of 445 academics in the United States by the Heterodox Academy found that 'more than half the respondents consider expressing views beyond a certain consensus in an academic setting quite dangerous to their career trajectory'. See John McWhorter, 'Academics are really, really worried about their freedom', the *Atlantic* (1 September 2020).

p.61 *'not exposed to intolerant or offensive ideas':* Kelsey Ann Naughton, *Speaking Freely: What Students Think About Expression at American Colleges* (Philadelphia: Foundation for Individual Rights in Education, November 2017), p. 3.

NOTES

p.61 **A video of the confrontation went viral:** For a fuller account of the Christakis affair, see Claire Fox, *I Find That Offensive!* (London: Biteback, 2016), pp. 57–67.

p.62 **colleagues were too frightened to risk defending them in public:** Erika Christakis, 'My Hallowe'en email led to a campus firestorm – and a troubling lesson about self-censorship', the *Washington Post* (28 October 2016).

p.62 **holding members of staff hostage:** Lukianoff and Haidt, op. cit., pp. 114–119.

p.62 **academic innovation depends upon those who do not conform:** The correlation between innovation and eccentricity is explored further by Geoffrey Miller in his article 'The neurodiversity case for free speech', *Quillette* (18 July 2017).

p.62 **'genius, mental vigour, and moral courage':** Mill, op. cit., p. 65.

p.63 **'a critique of conventional knowledge and the search for the new':** Joanna Williams, *Academic Freedom in an Age of Conformity: Confronting the Fear of Knowledge* (London: Palgrave Macmillian, 2016), p. 5.

p.63 **'struggle between Liberty and Authority':** Mill, op. cit., p. 5.

Persuasion and Debate

p.66 **Joseph Goebbels and Theodor Fritsch were prosecuted for their anti-Semitism:** As A Alan Borovoy of the Canadian Civil Liberties Association has pointed out, '[d]uring the fifteen years before Hitler came to power, there were more than two hundred prosecutions based on anti-Semitic speech. And, in the opinion of the leading Jewish organisation of that era, no more than 10 per cent of the cases were mishandled by the authorities. As subsequent history so painfully testifies, this type of legislation proved ineffectual on the one occasion when there was a real argument for it.' See A Alan Borovoy, *When Freedoms Collide: The Case for Our Civil Liberties* (Toronto: Lester and Orpen Dennys, 1988), p. 50.

p.66 **the cases 'served as effective public-relations machinery':** Bob Mankoff, 'Copenhagen, speech, and violence', the *New Yorker* (14 February 2015). In this piece, Mankoff interviews Flemming Rose, the foreign editor of *Jyllands-Posten*, a Danish publication which became the target of mass protests and threats having printed cartoons of the Prophet Mohammed in 2005.

p.66 **prosecutions for insults, contentious opinions and even jokes:** There have been numerous investigations and prosecutions for jokes in the UK in recent years.

In 2016, former footballer Paul Gascoigne was found guilty in a criminal court of racially aggravated abuse after a joke he made during his show *An Evening With Gazza* at Wolverhampton Civic Hall.

In 2018, Markus Meechan – known on YouTube as Count Dankula – was found guilty at Airdrie Sheriff Court in 2018 for the crime of hate speech and breaching the Communications Act. His arrest followed a viral online video in which Meechan can be seen encouraging his girlfriend's pug to give a Nazi salute and to respond enthusiastically to the phrases 'Sieg Heil' and 'gas the Jews'. Even though the intention behind the video was unambiguously comedic, and no evidence of far-right or racist sympathies was produced, Meechan was found guilty and sentenced to pay a fine of £800.

Even more established comedians have been the subject of police scrutiny. In 2019, Jo Brand was investigated and 'assessed' by the police for making jokes about throwing battery acid at politicians.

In Canada in 2016, Mike Ward was fined $42,000 by the Quebec Human Rights Tribunal for telling a joke about a disabled boy.

I have discussed these cases in various articles for *spiked*: 'Policing punchlines' (9 March 2016), 'The state's war on amateur comedians' (23 September 2016), 'The curious case of the Nazi pug' (10 July 2017), 'Count Dankula and the fall of liberal Britain' (12 October 2018) and 'Get the cops out of comedy' (17 June 2019). I also produced a television documentary about the Count Dankula case for the BBC entitled *The Nazi Pug: Joke or Hate?* (directed by Dan Murdoch).

p.67 *'any subject that was not to their palate'*: Milton, op. cit., p. 584.

p.67 *how can we be sure that our government will not pivot into similarly hyperbolic territory?*: Laurie Penny, *Bitch Doctrine: Essays for Dissenting Adults* (London: Bloomsbury, 2017), p. 41. Labour MEP Julie Ward, Twitter (14 June 2019).

p.68 *'No Platformed on that basis'*: The feminist Julie Bindel, for instance, has been repeatedly disinvited from UK universities for her gender-critical stance.

Words and Violence

p.69 *'the ground will become fertile for violence'*: Quoted by Saraya Wintersmith, 'If two enemies are talking, they're not fighting,' *Richmond Magazine* (16 March 2018).

p.69 *'All war represents a failure of diplomacy'*: Quoted by Brian Brivati, 'Tony Benn obituary', the *Guardian* (14 March 2014).

p.69 *refrain from inviting potentially controversial speakers to the campus*: Alex Morey and Samantha Harris, 'In anti-intellectual email, Wellesley profs call engaging with controversial arguments an imposition on students,' *FIRE* (21 March 2017).

p.70 **the cultivation of 'safe spaces' on university campuses:** Lukianoff and Haidt, op. cit., pp. 19–32.

p.70 **anything that causes emotional distress can be deemed traumatic:** Lukianoff and Haidt observe that the notion of 'safe spaces' in higher education was virtually unknown until 2015 when the *New York Times* published Judith Shulevitz's article 'In college and hiding from scary ideas'. Ibid., p. 26.

p.70 **'it seems that speech . . . can be a form of violence':** Lisa Feldman Barrett, 'When is speech violence?', the *New York Times* (14 July 2017).

p.71 **activists are able to justify censorship as a form of self-defence:** A similar effect is achieved by promoting the spurious idea that power differentials always corrupt the debating process, and that marginalised people are likely to be 'traumatised' by speaking in such an 'imbalanced' setting.

p.71 **acts of physical violence are 'acceptable':** 'Almost one in five students surveyed in a 2017 Brookings Institution study agreed that using violence to prevent a speaker from speaking was sometimes "acceptable". While some critics challenged the sampling used in that study, findings in a second study by McLaughlin and Associates were similar; 30 per cent of undergraduate students surveyed agreed with this statement: "If someone is using hate speech or making racially charged comments, physical violence can be justified to prevent this person from espousing their hateful views."' Lukianoff and Haidt, op. cit., p. 86.

p.72 **whether or not it was ethical to punch a Nazi:** Tauriq Moosa, 'The "punch a Nazi" meme: what are the ethics of punching Nazis?', the *Guardian* (31 January 2017).

p.72 **increasingly unpredictable cycles of conflict:** Hannah Arendt, *On Violence* (London: Allen Lane, 1969), p. 4.

p.72 **'an assault on an ideology':** See Adam Gopnik's foreword to Charbonnier, op. cit., pp. vii–xiii.

Identity Quakes

p.73 **We have all felt that sensation of disquietude:** A 2016 study found that most people perceive challenges to their political beliefs to be personal attacks. See Jonas T Kaplan, Sarah I Gimbel and Sam Harris, 'Neural correlates of maintaining one's political beliefs in the face of counter-evidence', *Scientific Reports* 6, 39589 (2016).

p.74 *'unsettled by the dinosaurs he found entombed in rock':* Tom Holland, *Dominion: How the Christian Revolution Remade the World* (New York: Basic Books, 2019), p. 437.

p.74 *the ichneumon wasp:* Ibid., p. 439.

p.74 *Darwin's Christian identity was shaken:* Hazlitt put it this way: 'Let any one, for instance, have been brought up in an opinion, let him have remained in it all his life, let him have attached all his notions of respectability, of the approbation of his fellow-citizens or his own self-esteem to it, let him then first hear it called in question and a strong and unforeseen objection stated to it, will not this startle and shock him as if he had seen a spectre, and will he not struggle to resist the arguments that would unsettle his habitual convictions, as he would resist the divorcing of soul and body?' He contended that in such moments 'bias of the will' would typically prevail over empirical evidence. Hazlitt, *Literary Remains,* op, cit., pp. 84–86.

p.74 *'identity quakes':* Boghossian and Lindsay, op. cit., p. 167.

p.74 *life is by necessity punctuated with these little shocks of awakening:* Jordan Peterson sums this up as follows: 'Every bit of learning is a little death. Every bit of new information challenges a previous conception, forcing it to dissolve into chaos before it can be reborn as something better. Sometimes such deaths virtually destroy us.' Jordan Peterson, *12 Rules for Life: an Antidote to Chaos* (London: Allen Lane, 2018), p. 223.

p.74 *'Don't feel harmed – and you haven't been':* Marcus Aurelius, *Meditations* (New York: Modern Library, 2002), trans. Gregory Hays, p. 39.

p.75 *I would be the one guilty of encroaching on the liberty of another:* 'The only freedom which deserves the name, is that of pursuing our own good in our own way, so long as we do not attempt to deprive others of theirs, or impede their efforts to obtain it.' Mill, op. cit., p. 15.

p.75 *'a general drama of pain':* Thomas Hardy, *The Mayor of Casterbridge* (Oxford: Oxford University Press, 1987), p. 335. Originally published in 1886.

Incitement

p.78 *triggered a reaction in those predisposed to act violently:* As Milton put it, 'Evil manners are as perfectly learnt without books a thousand other ways which cannot be stopped.' Milton, op. cit., p. 592.

p.79 *angry students accosted Chelsea Clinton:* Adam Forrest, 'Chelsea Clinton confronted by angry students claiming New Zealand massacre was "stoked by people like you"', the *Independent* (16 March 2019).

p.79 ***the killer had recently shared an article from the* Daily Express:** Owen Jones, Twitter (15 March 2019).

p.79 ***when the intention to incite violence is beyond doubt:*** This is certainly the view of the Scottish National Party, whose Hate Crime and Public Order Bill (2020) was ostensibly proposed to repeal outdated measures against blasphemy, but instead amounts to an ushering in of a range of new blasphemy laws by stealth. Most controversially, part two of the Bill pertains to the offence of 'stirring up hatred', which criminalises anyone who 'behaves in a threatening, abusive or insulting manner' or 'communicates threatening, abusive or insulting material to another person'. In its original form, the bill had criminalised the stirring up of hatred even if there had been no intention to do so, but this was amended following a backlash from civil liberties campaigners.

p.81 ***'beliefs that lead to costly behaviour are even less likely to be accepted':*** Hugo Mercier, 'How gullible are we? A review of the evidence from Psychology and Social Science', *Review of General Psychology* vol. 21, issue 2 (June 2017), pp. 103–122.

p.81 ***propaganda had the reverse impact:*** Maja Adena, Ruben Enikolopov, Maria Petrova, Veronica Santarosa and Ekaterina Zhuravskaya, 'Radio and the rise of the Nazis in prewar Germany', the *Quarterly Journal of Economics*, vol. 13, issue 4 (November 2015), pp. 1885–1939.

p.81 ***'people who are already hateful and prone to violence':*** Gordon Danning, '"Hate speech" does not incite hatred', *Quillette* (18 January 2018).

p.81 ***the current movement in the United States to see that hate speech is exempt:*** Writing in the *New York Times*, Emily Bazelon argues that the First Amendment is ill-equipped to deal with 'the spread of viral disinformation' in the digital age. See Emily Bazelon, 'The problem with free speech in an age of disinformation', the *New York Times* (18 October 2020).

p.82 ***Marantz's strategy of recasting his argument as a 'fact':*** In Robby Soave's rebuttal to Marantz's article, he points out that rates of violent crime in the US have continually fallen since the 1990s, even though during that same period the Supreme Court has been increasingly insistent on upholding protections guaranteed by the First Amendment. And in spite of the growing threat of white nationalism, domestic terrorism represents only a tiny proportion of violent crime statistics. If it were true that free speech leads to violence, we would expect to see this reflected in the numbers. See Robby Soave, 'The *New York Times* says "free speech is killing us" but violent crime is lower than ever', *Reason* (4 October 2019).

p.83 ***'Books are well written, or badly written. That is all':*** Wilde, op. cit., pp. 129–320. Quotation taken from p. 129.

p.83 *the seizure of so-called 'video nasties'*: Quoted by Sarah Cleary, '"Maggot maladies": origins of horror as a culturally proscribed entertainment', Kevin Corstorphine and Laura R Kremmel (eds.), in *The Palgrave Handbook to Horror Literature* (London: Palgrave Macmillan, 2018), pp. 391–406. Quotation taken from p. 392.

p.84 **Trainspotting** *(1996) was accused of glamourising drug use:* John Arlidge, 'Drugs films attacked for glamorising heroin', the *Independent* (16 February 1996).

p.84 **Crash** *(1996) banned in the UK:* Tom Fordy, '"Britain still has a repressive strain": David Cronenberg on his "depraved" classic, Crash', the *Telegraph* (10 November 2020).

p.84 *'a toxic rallying cry for self-pitying incels'*: David Ehrlich, '*Joker* review: for better or worse, superhero movies will never be the same', *IndieWire* (31 August 2019). The term 'incel' is short for 'involuntary celibate'; it is a form of self-identification for mostly young heterosexual men who have difficulty finding sexual partners, and has become associated with misogynistic online behaviour.

p.84 *'I would rather give a healthy boy or a healthy girl a phial of prussic acid'*: James Douglas, 'A book that must be suppressed', *Sunday Express* (19 August 1928).

p.84 *'direct-effects model'*: Ralph A Hanson has described how research undertaken after the Second World War 'looking for powerful direct effects leading to opinion and behavioural changes generally came up short. In fact, in the 1940s and 1950s, researchers sometimes doubted whether media messages had any effect on individuals at all.' He notes that the direct-effects model fails to view media messages 'as a stimulus that would lead to a predictable attitudinal or behavioural response with nothing intervening between sender and audience', and that the indirect-effects approach, by contrast, recognises that 'audience members perceive and interpret these messages selectively according to individual differences'. Ralph E Hanson, *Mass Communication: Living in a Media World* (Washington, DC: CQ Press, 2011), pp. 47–48.

p.84 *such effects are only ever indirect:* The same is true of sexual violence; studies repeatedly show that incidents of rape and sexual assault are not exacerbated when there is increased access to pornographic material. For a brief overview of various international studies, see Michael Castleman, 'Evidence Mounts: More Porn, Less Sexual Assault', *Psychology Today* (14 January 2016).

p.85 *the 'Streisand effect'*: The 'Streisand effect' is named after the singer Barbra Streisand, who in 2003 filed a lawsuit against a photographer who had published a photograph of her home in Malibu in order to document coastal erosion. The subsequent publicity ultimately drew considerable attention to the very image that Streisand hoped to suppress.

Hate Speech

p.87   **'hate speech' is not something that can be meaningfully defined:** In 2012, the European Court of Human Rights concluded that there 'is no universally accepted definition of the expression "hate speech"', and a manual published by UNESCO in 2015 accepted that 'the possibility of reaching a universally shared definition seems unlikely'. Quoted by Paul Coleman, *Censored: How European 'Hate Speech' Laws are Threatening Freedom of Speech*, second edition (Vienna: Kairos Publications, 2016), p. 5. Alexander Brown has also noted that the jurisprudential literature on hate speech 'contains numerous competing, sometimes contradictory characterizations'. See Alexander Brown, *Hate Speech Law: A Philosophical Examination* (London: Routledge, 2017), p. 4.

p.87   **all European countries have hate-speech laws:** Coleman, op. cit., p. 11.

p.88   **guidelines by the Crown Prosecution Service define 'hate crime':** *Hate Crime: What It Is and How to Support Victims and Witnesses*, Crown Prosecution Service (October 2016).

p.88   **'hate incident' is defined as a non-criminal act:** This quotation is taken from the UK government's website on 'hate crime'.

p.88   **College of Policing instructs officers to record hateful incidents:** *Hate Crime Operational Guidance* (Coventry: College of Policing, 2014), p. 61.

p.89   **the criminalisation of speech in private dwellings:** Mark McLaughlin, 'Hate crime bill: hate talk in homes "must be prosecuted"', the *Times* (28 October 2020). In an address in the House of Commons in March 1763, William Pitt the Elder (1708–78) recognised that the home is a sanctuary for every citizen in which even treasonous sentiments might be safely expressed: 'The poorest man may in his cottage bid defiance to all the forces of the Crown. It may be frail, its roof may shake, the wind may blow through it, the storm may enter, the rain may enter, but the King of England cannot enter. All his force dares not cross the threshold of the ruined tenement.'

p.89   **a joke had clearly been intended:** Charlie Parker, 'Police arresting nine people a day in fight against web trolls', the *Times* (12 October 2017).

p.89   **intention to cause offence:** One of the more disturbing aspects of the authoritarian drift of recent years has been the suggestion that intention should be disregarded in circumstances in which someone has taken offence. The new discourse of 'microaggressions' – unthinking comments that occur in day-to-day interactions which can be insensitive to marginalised groups – has had the effect of promoting the idea that 'aggression' is unrelated to intent. Such a view completely destabilises our view of morality, and can be advanced to justify draconian strictures on speech. See for instance Anna Liu's comment in her article 'No You're Not Imagining It: 3 Ways Racial Microaggressions Sneak into Our Lives' for *Everyday Feminism* (25 February 2015): 'It's important for us to remember that just because a perpetrator of racism is clueless (or in denial) about the impact of their words, doesn't mean that their actions were any less violent or that the impact of that violence is changed. When it comes down to it, intention is irrelevant.'

p.89   *legal action under Ontario's human rights code:* Jason McBride, 'The Pronoun Warrior', *Toronto Life* (25 January 2017).

p.90   *police investigations into 'misgendering':* In February 2018, a schoolteacher was told by police that she had committed a 'hate crime' for misgendering one of her pupils. The matter was eventually resolved when the school agreed to provide more diversity training for its staff.

In March 2019, journalist Caroline Farrow was contacted by the police for using the pronoun 'he' in reference to a person who identifies as female during an appearance on ITV's *Good Morning Britain*.

In February 2020, Kate Scottow was convicted under the Communications Act for insulting and misgendering a trans person on Twitter. She was apparently arrested in front of her children and confined to a cell for seven hours. She has since been cleared following a successful appeal against her conviction.

See Camilla Turner, 'Teacher accused of "misgendering" child was told by police that she committed a hate crime', the *Telegraph* (23 February 2018); Martin Evans and Gabriella Swerling, 'Devout Catholic "who used wrong pronoun to describe transgender girl" to be interviewed by police', the *Telegraph* (20 March 2019); Kim Thomas, 'I stand with Kate Scottow', the *Spectator* (14 February 2020).

p.90   *'this prospect frightens me much more than bombs':* George Orwell, 'Looking back on the Spanish war', in Davison, op. cit., pp. 431–451. Quotation taken from p. 442. In Orwell's dystopian novel *Nineteen Eighty-Four* (1949), the Ministry of Truth – a division of the ruling party Ingsoc – repeatedly proclaims self-contradictory slogans: 'war is peace', 'freedom is slavery' and 'ignorance is strength'. In his diary, Winston Smith writes: 'Freedom is the freedom to say that two plus two make four. If that is granted, all else follows.' By the end of the novel, his resolve has been entirely diminished under torture, and he finds himself unconsciously tracing the equation '2+2=5' in the dust on a table. George Orwell, *Nineteen Eighty-Four* (London: Penguin, 1987), p. 84 and p. 303.

p.90   *'the master of his own thoughts':* RHM Elwes (trans.), *The Chief Works of Benedict de Spinoza*, 2 vols. (London: Chiswick Press, 1883), vol. I, p. 258.

NOTES

Year Zero

p.93   *ambitions seem inimical to the organisation's* **raison d'être:** Chase
Strangio, the ACLU's Deputy Director for Transgender Justice of its LGBT
& HIV Project, recently expressed his support for 'stopping the circulation'
of Abigail Shrier's book *Irreversible Damage: The Transgender Craze Seducing
Our Daughters* (Washington, DC: Regnery Publishing, 2020). See Abigail
Shrier, 'Does the ACLU want to ban my book?', the *Wall Street Journal* (15
November 2020).

p.94   *burning copies of Salman Rushdie's novel:* Salman Rushdie was subjected
to a *fatwa* – a death sentence pronounced by the Supreme Leader of Iran,
Ayatollah Khomeini – because his novel *The Satanic Verses* was deemed to
be blasphemous against Islam.

p.94   *the crowd would not have hesitated to see him suffer:* The singer Yusuf
Islam, formerly known as Cat Stevens, made this feeling explicit in an
appearance on the Australian television show *Hypotheticals*. The host
Geoffrey Robertson asked him whether he would attend a demonstration
where an effigy of Rushdie was to be burned. In response, Islam said, 'I
would have hoped that it'd be the real thing.'

p.94   *'now the victory of the Enlightenment was looking temporary, reversible':*
Salman Rushdie, *Joseph Anton* (London: Jonathan Cape, 2012), pp. 128–129.

p.94   *where they burn books:* In Milton's *Areopagitica*, the destruction of books
is likened to a form of homicide, 'whereof the execution ends not in the
slaying of an elemental life, but strikes at that ethereal and fifth essence,
the breath of reason itself, slays an immortality rather than a life'. Milton,
op. cit., p. 579.

p.94   *making martyrs out of reprehensible people:* 'If all mankind minus one
were of one opinion, and only one person were of the contrary opinion,
mankind would be no more justified in silencing that one person, than he,
if he had the power, would be justified in silencing mankind.' Mill, op. cit.,
pp. 18–19.

p.95   *debate is not, as some have asserted, a 'fetish':* For example, see Nadia
Whittome, 'The only way to avoid hysteria about trans rights is to ground
the debate in real life experiences,' the *Independent* (23 July 2020), in
which it is claimed that 'we must not fetishise "debate" as though debate is
itself an innocuous, neutral act'.

p.95   *much of the received wisdom of the present will be derided by our descendants:* 'All silencing of discussion is an assumption of infallibility.'
Mill, op. cit., p. 19. See also Milton, op. cit., p. 593: 'How shall the licensers
themselves be confided in, unless we can confer upon them, or they assume

to themselves above all others in the land, the grace of infallibility and uncorruptedness?'

p.95 **'the Right of every Man to his own opinion':** Quoted by Christopher Hitchens, *Thomas Paine's Rights of Man: A Biography* (Vancouver: Douglas & McIntyre, 2006), p. 123.

p.95 **the 'outdated notion' of Western civilisation:** Craig Simpson, 'Exclusive: British Library's chief librarian claims "racism is the creation of white people"', the *Telegraph* (29 August 2020).

p.96 **monuments to Mahatma Gandhi and Abraham Lincoln:** In London, there have been consultations about whether statues and other landmarks, including street names, should be modified in accordance with today's values. This kind of government-sanctioned revisionism is reminiscent of Winston's words in George Orwell's *Nineteen Eighty-Four*: 'Every record has been destroyed or falsified, every book has been rewritten, every picture has been repainted, every statue and street and building has been renamed, every date has been altered. And that process is continuing day by day and minute by minute. History has stopped.' Op. cit., p. 162.

p.97 **these are already illegal and require no additional legislation:** Nadine Strossen cites an article by Amos Guiora – 'In this age of Internet hate, it's time to revisit limits on free speech,' the *Salt Lake Tribune* (4 December 2016) – to show how calls for tighter hate-speech laws are often justified by acts that are already criminal. For instance, Guiora mentions the example of white nationalists who spray-painted swastikas on to a school door. Strossen points out that this is an act of vandalism, which is illegal, irrespective of the content of the message. Similarly, a note left on a Jewish professor's home that read 'Gas Jews Die' violates existing constitutional protections against the issuing of threats. 'In sum,' writes Strossen, 'all but one of the situations that Guiora cites as ostensibly supporting the need to "revisit limits on free speech" instead prove the opposite: that existing free speech principles permit outlawing and punishing the actions to which he (understandably) objects.' See Nadine Strossen, *Hate: Why We Should Resist It with Free Speech, Not Censorship* (Oxford: Oxford University Press, 2018), pp. 54–56.

p.97 **the 'gramophone mind':** George Orwell, 'The freedom of the press', in Davison, op. cit., pp. 888 –897. Quotation taken from p. 896. The essay was originally written as a preface to Orwell's novel *Animal Farm* (London: Secker & Warburg, 1945), but was not published until the typescript was posthumously discovered in 1972.

p.97 **we only enfeeble ourselves if we neglect to use them:** Quoted by Joseph Schumpeter, *Capitalism, Socialism and Democracy*, fourth edition (London: George Allen & Unwin Ltd, 1954), p. 12. First edition published in 1943.

Index